ENDURE

ENDURE

a christian man's guide to

FINISHING STRONG

BILL NEWTON

This is what I would expect from my friend, Bill Newton. A thoroughly biblical and intensely practical call to "press on toward the goal for the prize of the upward call of God in Christ Jesus." It provides enough of a challenge to keep us from lethargy and plenty of encouragement to run with all the strength that God provides, now that we see the finishing line in view.

ALISTAIR BEGG: *Senior Pastor of Parkside Church and voice behind the "Truth For Life" radio preaching and teaching ministry, which broadcasts his sermons daily to stations across North America through over 1,800 radio outlets. He is also the author or co-author of ten books from several publishers.*

This 18,000-word book contains more protein than most 80,000-word volumes. Bill Newton shows with good specifics and stories what it means to finish strong. His lessons include: *Look for progress and not perfection, Be willing to die to self,* and *Focus on what you can become.* In a "do your own thing era," Newton's emphasis on becoming less independent, and more dependent on God, is crucial.

MARVIN OLASKY: *Former Editor in Chief, World Magazine and World News Group, Former Dean of the World Journalism Institute, and the author of twenty-six books*

Finishing Strong is a term used often in our culture, mostly associated with everything except our faith. The news media reminds us daily of those who have missed the goal. Bill Newton, in this book, gives a biblically correct, clear, and concise plan of action. His encouraging, direct, and challenging exhortation for Christian men to grow in their faith and knowledge of our Lord and Savior Jesus Christ, *Endure,* is a wake-up call for Christian men to live lives worthy and pleasing to God.

ANDRE THORNTON: *Former professional baseball player, a two-time All-star, with a fourteen-year big league career with the Chicago Cubs, Montreal Expos, and Cleveland Indians; author of Triumph Born of Tragedy published by Harvest House*

I was sobered to read that, according to Dr. J. Robert Clinton of Fuller Theological Seminary, as many as 70 percent of leaders, biblically and historically, do not finish well. That data alone was enough to propel me to read this powerful little book. I found what I'd hoped for. A companion on the journey from a trusted, proven leader, a good friend who has consistently walked the talk. With its rich insights you, too, will be better equipped to finish strong and fulfill God's purposes for your life.

JOHN BECKETT: Chairman and primary owner of The Beckett Companies, R.W. Beckett, Beckett Gas, Beckett Air, Beckett, Canada, Beckett Asia-Pacific, and author of Loving Monday: Succeeding in Business without Selling Your Soul (translated into nineteen languages); The War Letters; and Mastering Monday

No one should pick up this little book with the expectation of finding a short list of catch-up techniques for doing late in life what you should have done earlier. To be sure, if that's you, there's plenty of help here. But Bill Newton's too committed to the fullness of Scripture to engage in proof-texting. Wherever you are in your spiritual walk, you'll appreciate Newton's well-structured approach. If you're like me, you're likely to say, "I could use that."

JOEL BELZ: Founder of God's World Publications which includes the World Magazine, World Journalism Institute, The World and Everything in It podcast, World Watch video, a daily news outlet for kids and youth, and World Kids, World Teen, God's Big World. Joel has had a published column in almost every edition of World Magazine since it began in 1986. He was also the thirty-first Moderator of the PCA General Assembly.

Bill shows us, step by step, how to commit to finishing strong. Every lesson Bill teaches is supported by specific Scripture and explained by real-world examples. Additionally, he points out the importance of knowing all Scripture, not just the parts we like best. This is the easiest book to understand God's plan for each one of us to finish strong.

BILL TRUAX: Owner of TRUFIELD ENTERPRISES, Inc., a firm that taught Goal Achievement skills to individuals as well as Sales, Management, and Project teams and co-author with his wife Susie of The BLITZ CALL®, A System for Fear Free Prospecting and Making Cold Calls, and three more books on prospecting, as well as two CDs

ENDURE
A Christian Man's Guide to Finishing Strong
Revised and Expanded Edition

Bill Newton

Copyright © 2022 Bill Newton

ISBNS:
Paper: 978-1-63342-294-0
ePub: 978-1-63342-296-4
mobi: 978-1-63342-297-1

Cover design and typeset by www.greatwriting.org

Printed in Colombia

Shepherd Press
P.O. Box 24
Wapwallopen, PA 18660
www.shepherdpress.com

Acknowledgments

• • • • • • • • • • • • • • • • • •

I would like to say that I've been thinking about this book for years. However that would be a lie. My Administrative Assistant, Pat Leahy, is the genesis for this book. He dug out old materials I had used years earlier for seminars and talks to men and he convinced me that the material would be useful for men of all ages. Next, he initiated contact with publishers and then tirelessly edited every word in the book. He deserves credit for the entire project.

There are numerous other people whom I need to thank. Tom Petersburg read the initial draft and offered incredible insights and additions. His knowledge, empathy, and wisdom concerning men and their issues is invaluable. Jim Bzdafka and John Beckett also read the original drafts, and meticulously provided encouragement and advice about how men might actually use the book. John Beckett's real-world experience with applying biblical principles in business is unsurpassed. Marvin Olasky has encouraged me to write for a number of years. His advice and counsel, as well as guidance on telling stories, has been invaluable. His willingness to spend time on my project is greatly appreciated. Dan Donovan from *Family Life* gave me useful and helpful direction on how to proceed, especially what publishers might be best.

There are six people who read the draft and agreed to give endorsements. Their encouragement and words provided the motivation to stick to the project and keep going. These six men were Marvin Olasky, Joel Belz, Andre Thornton, John Beckett, Bill Truax, and Alistair Begg. All of these men are men of substance and respect, and their achievements are substantial. Their collective influence on my thinking cannot be overstated.

I would be remiss if I did not acknowledge the impact that sitting under Alistair Begg's preaching for almost twenty years has had on my life and thinking. Thinking biblically is the genesis for righteous living. I got that genesis under Alistair's tutelage. In a similar fashion, *World Magazine* and its outstanding Board has helped me think though how biblical theology applies to all aspects of our culture. God is interested in every part of our culture and our lives. I would have never gained these benefits had it not been for Joel Belz. His friendship and invitation to come and see what *World* was all about and join the Board began our relationship.

I gladly recognize the contributions that my family have made to this project. My son and daughter, Michael Newton and Kristine Sung, have read drafts and advised their Dad with loving constructive criticism. My wife, Linda, has endured reading draft after draft of every chapter, and has tolerated discussions of alternatives until she was spent. Without her loving encouragement to continue, and Pat Leahy's faithful prodding, this project would have died a slow death.

Jim Holmes from Shepherd Press has lived up to the publisher's name, being a godly shepherd all the way. His advice, ideas, and knowledge of the business of publishing have been invaluable. Shepherd Press's willingness to take a risk on an aged, unknown author is also gutsy and appreciated.

Finally, I would be remiss if I did not thank God Almighty. He has provided my salvation, all the people who have helped me along the way, and has guided the process. He has given me teaching from some of the best most gifted preachers and Christian writers that are alive today. My prayer is that this project may bring Him glory and impact men positively to endure and live godly lives.

Foreword

• • • • • • • • • • • •

On a Sunday morning in Cleveland, Bill Newton spoke at chapel for both Major League baseball teams between their batting practice and the first pitch. As professional athletes are drawn to speakers who have excelled in sports and risked their lives catapulting off aircraft carriers, Bill had an open lane to talk about making Jesus the priority of their lives and careers.

About twenty years later, Bill was my speaker at an annual forum for businessmen who gathered to focus on influence as Christian men. His topic was *Finishing Strong*. The men in the room were hooked before Bill nailed his first point. When the session ended, one of the men pulled me aside with a look of excitement and said, "That guy speaks my language."

Over the years, I have reflected on what God did in men's lives in these events through Bill. My conclusions always came back to two things: the *message* and the *messenger*.

The *message* of endurance and finishing strong resonates with men. They know that finishing strong is not automatic. They know Christian leaders who have failed miserably in their final laps of the race, so they feel vulnerable. If the guys on the platform fail so often, what hope is there for the guys in the pew? They know that good intentions won't cut it, so they are looking for some serious insights.

The message of this book, enduring to finish strong, is based on clear, biblical truths and the testimony of biblical characters. You can't miss Bill's conclusions: God intends to finish the work He has begun in us (Philippians 1:6), but it requires us taking steps to develop new patterns in our lives.

Bill is an encouraging *messenger*. He is finishing his own race with endurance, but knows that he is not finished. He identifies with the same struggles, dilemmas, and decisions that most men face. His attitude reveals a personal need for

Jesus no different from the men who are just coming out of the starting blocks. Therefore, the message is delivered with grace and hope.

Bill speaks and writes from a unique perspective. He illustrates truths that have been tested and proven in the crucible of life as an athlete, naval aviator, employee, executive, entrepreneur, corporate consultant, seminary professor, church planter, and pastor. That is why men will find the content of this study conveyed in their language.

It doesn't really matter how far you are in your own race of life. If you are running well, you will be strengthened by the reminders, warnings, and directions of the Scriptures. This study will also give you another resource for the men you seek to encourage in the faith.

In Galatians 5:7, Paul says to believers who have gotten off track because of legalism, of merely performing for God's approval, "You were running well; who hindered you from obeying the truth?" If you have stumbled, given up hope, or have taken a detour, the truth and grace in these pages will lead you back to deal with the heart issues of your relationship with God.

Finishing strong may not be a guarantee, but this guide offers an effective pattern.

Tom Petersburg
(Former Chaplain to Cleveland professional sports teams)

Introduction

Do you not know that in a race all the runners run, but only one receives the prize? So run that you may obtain it. Every athlete exercises self-control in all things. They do it to receive a perishable wreath, but we an imperishable. So I do not run aimlessly; I do not box as one beating the air. But I discipline my body and keep it under control, lest after preaching to others I myself should be disqualified.
1 Corinthians 9:24–27

Jesse was in his forties and had a successful track record as a crackerjack salesman and executive in several Fortune 1000 companies. His success led him to start his own business. His desire was to found and run his company on biblical principles and commit part of the profits to Christian missions.

The company grew and profits came, and Christian missions benefitted. Over time, however, the principles of Christian ethics remained in writing, but the operating activities began to veer from the desired targets. Why this happened is anyone's guess, but, for many observers, the facts of the decline left disappointment in their wake—high staff turnover at the company, disillusionment for what it meant to be a Christian, and a cynicism about a business run on Christian principles.

Catastrophic Moral Failure
⋄⋄

By the time Jesse was in his late sixties, things began to get tougher and, for reasons no one understands, Jesse had a severe moral failure that led to his resignation as CEO, a sale of the company at its nadir, and embarrassment for the cause of Christianity. Many said it would have been better if the company had never claimed to be operating on Christian principles. Jesse was (and still is) a good friend, but his failure caused me to begin thinking about what it takes to finish the race of life growing in the graces of Christ instead of stumbling into sin. For Jesse, life is not over—he can recover, and I hope he does—but damage has been done.

The recently exposed moral failures uncovered by the law firm investigating Ravi Zacharias, and the failure of Jesse, put an exclamation mark on my desire to think through what it means to endure and finish a life and career well. My administrative assistant, Pat Leahy, dug out some old notes from materials I used at a men's retreat for a church in Portland, Oregon, and later at a ministry in Cleveland, Ohio. The subject of those presentations was "finishing strong." After Pat read the materials, he vehemently urged me to put the material in book form. This book is an attempt to do just what Pat suggested—put in writing what I covered verbally at those retreats.

Principles
◇◇◇◇◇◇◇◇◇◇◇◇◇◇◇◇◇◇

This book is not a biography or a narrative that flows from one day to the next or year to year. It is a collection of principles learned from godly teachers and preachers, and a life filled with athletic, military, business, family, mission-field, and pastoral experiences. All these principles and experiences point to the importance of "endurance" in running life's race to the finish. Paul put it this way as he addressed the Philippian church: "Not that I have already obtained this or am already perfect, but I press on to make it my own, because Christ Jesus has made me his own" (Phil. 3:12).

My hope is that this material will help young men prepare for the finish line, equip faithful Christian men with challenges to help them grow, and prevent any other people like Jesse out there from failing as they approach the finish. When men like Ravi and Jesse fail in their later years, especially from some moral failure, a whole lifetime's reputation can be destroyed and, more importantly, the cause of the Kingdom becomes dishonored.

But more important than these high-profile leaders are the millions of Christian men leading their families, their work associates, and their friends in the course of everyday life. I am not a high-profile personality, yet I influence my brothers and sisters, my grown children, my grandchildren, my wife, my cousins and extended family, my neighbors, my in-laws, my fellow church members, my friends at our former churches, my former work associates, my classmates from USNA and Harvard, my former teammates in baseball, basketball, football, and the men and women that I have mentored and counseled. I hope you get the idea. I am a "nobody" and yet the total number of people that might be negatively impacted by my finishing poorly is a large number. My guess is, if you think about it, we all have a fairly large number of people watching our example. Living well, enduring well, and finishing strongly are all important.

But a singular focus on preventing failure alone is a strategy that leads to a poor finish. Preventing failure is a defensive strategy. To win football games, a championship team needs to have both a strong defense and a strong offense. The same is true with finishing strong. There are things we desire to prevent and avoid—those are defensive strategies. I deal with those in this book. There are also things we need to pursue, develop, nurture, and pray for. These are offensive strategies, and they are equally important. I also try to deal with those. A fearful overemphasis on defense without an appropriate attention to offense will lead to a dissatisfying outcome. Both are important, and both need our attention.

Failures on defense or offense begin on the inside, whether you are a famous personality or regular guy. Let there be no doubt about that! The roots of our failures are in our hearts. The Bible defines the heart as the center of our being as God's image bearers and includes the mind, the emotions, and the will of a believer. Beliefs drive the engine of our hearts, influenced by, regulated by, and responded to by our wills.

Proper beliefs begin in the mind and are tested by the trials of life. Those trials should lead to appropriate convictions of the heart. The convictions lead to suitable attitudes, and those attitudes then hopefully will translate into godly behaviors. This is why biblical knowledge, good theology, and accurate handling of the biblical text are so important. What we believe ultimately results in our willful actions. Belief leads to behavior.

An illustration may help. A curious young boy is warned by his mother not to touch the electric burners on a stove. The boy finds the beautiful red burners enticing. Attracted to them, he touches the glowing, round, hot elements. He cries, and his mom soothes his wounded spirit. He never touches the stove again. His belief begins by assuming his mom is wrong and stove rings are playthings. His belief is tested. That test produces a severely burnt finger and a conviction that his mom was right. His attitude toward stoves and his mom's word changes. His behavior now conforms with his tested belief.

Sustained righteousness is an internal matter. The suggestions in this book may seem to imply that certain actions alone are what are needed to finish strong. Nothing could be further from the truth. Sustained willpower is necessary, but not sufficient, for a proper finish. The heart of the matter is the human heart—real change and permanent change begin inside.

Change from the Inside Out

It is possible to willfully change your behavior in spurts. Isolated external actions for short periods of time are merely window dressings on a filthy, broken window. Christ called similar behaviors "white-washed tombs" as he addressed the external self-righteousness of the Pharisees. These tombs and behaviors look good on the outside for a period of time until the stench of death permeates their reality.

Let me be clear about this: I am after changing your mind and your thinking with proven ideas that have their origin in the Bible! The Bible is given to us to help us know who God is, what He has done in human history, and help us to understand how we may best relate to Him. My suggestions and warnings are not infallible, but their roots are in God's Word, and they are designed to help us think about what it means to finish strong. Not all suggestions are merely suggestions. My wife pointed out that the suggestion in chapter 2 (*You Must Be Born Again*) is not a suggestion at all. In fact, it is an absolute requirement. She is correct.

As you read this book, may God cause you to be like the Bereans that Paul commended in the book of Acts.

> Now these Jews were more noble than those in Thessalonica; they received the word with all eagerness, examining the Scriptures daily to see if these things were so.
> (Acts 17:11)

Please, examine these suggestions and see if they are so.

1

Take Your Finish Seriously

For we must all appear before the judgment seat of Christ, so that each one may receive what is due for what he has done in the body, whether good or evil.
2 Corinthians 5:10

Anyone running a race knows that it is as important to start quickly as it is to run fast and hard all the way through the finish line tape. Eric Liddell, the Scottish missionary to China, was knocked down in a 400-meter race shortly after the race began and by the time he regained his footing, the pack leader was more than thirty meters ahead.

Eric Liddell
➰➰➰➰➰➰➰➰➰➰➰

Most runners would have assumed the race was lost, but not Liddell. Liddell felt that his speed was a gift given to him by God. Using that gift was part of his life purpose, so he willed himself to continue the race, catching and passing the leaders in the last twenty meters—a task that most track coaches deemed impossible. Liddell collapsed from the physical exhaustion he willed his body to endure, and it is said that it took nine months to recover from the overexertion that he willed it to endure. One could argue that he finished the race - faster than he began it.

After his wins in the Olympics, Liddell went on to become a missionary to China, where he finished his earthly race as fast as he had the earlier 400-meter dash.

One key difference between life's race and any competitive race like track, swimming, or crew is this: in a competitive sports race, we know where the finish line is. In life's journey we do not know when we will finish or where. My three best friends, one from the Naval Academy, one from my flying days, and one from Harvard, all died within a span of six months and were in their thirties or forties. All were in good health, good shape, and all had successful careers. One died from a ski accident, hitting his head on a boulder and never coming out of the coma. One was healthy one day and the next day developed an aggressive melanoma cancer and died within a matter of a few weeks. The third was the pilot of the space shuttle *Challenger*, which exploded after seventy-three seconds of flight. The point is simple. We do not know when our finish will be, so this book is not just for old geezers like me, but for men of all ages.

Finishing the race of life spiritually faster than we began it—and doing so in a manner that brings glory to God—is what I mean by enduring well and finishing strong. This is extraordinarily important. The key heart motivation for this objective is captured in this short prayer.

God,
Please enable me to finish my life in a way that brings glory to you. Help me to avoid any moral failures that I know I am prone to wander into, enable me to cultivate my appetites for godly virtues, and give me the strength and wisdom to say no to those appetites that will harm me, my family, my church, my friends, my community, and, most importantly, You.

Search my heart and see if there is any evil way within me and give me the will and dependence on You to mortify that evil. Cultivate within me an ever-growing affection for You and relationship with You.

Give me the energy and stamina to run through life's finish line in a way that will please You and be useful to the Kingdom.

I want to finish strong!
In Christ's name I pray,
Amen.

Arthur Armour

One contemporary example of a man who endured to the end and finished well may help illustrate what I mean. Arthur Armour was a resident of a small town in Western Pennsylvania. I met him when I bought SATEC Systems. Art was seventy-nine years old at the time. He was not rich, he did not inherit a load of money, he never held political office, and he was never the pastor of a church.

Arthur was a talented artist who specialized in creating what was once called "Depression Silver." Depression Silver was handwrought aluminum, with intricate and beautiful designs etched into the surface. Arthur created quality pieces unique in style and valued by collectors. Art continued his artistic work until he died. But his artwork was not what endeared Art to me. Art was a committed believer. He befriended me and began to teach me theology over dinners that he cooked himself in his home. I learned much of my theology from this layman, sitting at his dinner table or basking in front of his coal-fired fireplace.

His first wife had died before I met Art and he lived alone, just blocks from Grove City College. On nights when he wasn't teaching me, he was serving dinner to college students, evangelizing them or discipling them, whichever was needed. He related equally to nineteen-year-olds, fifty-year-olds, and eighty-year-olds. His passion for Christ and solid theology was warm, sincere, well taught, and vocal. All who shared a meal at Art's house, whether they agreed with him or not, whether they became believers or not, experienced the aroma of Christ as they spent time with him. In a normal year, Art would share meals and theology with hundreds of students and mentees like me.

In his eighties, Art took a second wife, a lady quite some years younger than he was, and it was a pleasure to see them both together. Art designed and then acted as a general contractor to add a new master bedroom suite to his old home, so his new bride would not have to share a bedroom that wife number one had been in. The delight he had on his face as he showed me the completed addition to his home is etched on my brain.

After they were married, I took Art and his new bride to a marriage seminar led by Elisabeth Elliot, and they took a front row seat for the entire weekend. They were the center of attention and an example of fidelity to all who attended. Their plan for the marriage was that the new younger bride would outlive Art and take care of him in his old age. But as plans often do, things went awry. Bride number two became ill and abruptly died, and I empathized and experienced Art's grieving. He was wrought with pain and overcome at times with tears. Questions poured from his well-versed mind, and he was genuine in his honesty about his grief! Art's faith was tested, and it survived with edifying assurance for all who knew him. Through it all, his belief in the sovereignty of God was strengthened, not weakened, and his candid grieving taught me lessons.

Art died not long after that, and I was unable to attend the final service but I was told that the sanctuary at his church was filled with youngsters, family, friends, and church members—young and old. Each one had a story to tell of how Art had impacted his or her life for the cause of Christ. Tears were shed, but joy filled the place as people knew that Art was now with his Savior, whom he had for so long praised as his beloved. This unassuming, godly man finished strong. My hope and prayer is that I may someday follow the path that Art blazed, and that maybe this book will impact others to do the same.

2

◇◇◇◇◇◇◇◇◇◇◇◇

You Must Be Born Again

Jesus answered him, "Truly, truly, I say to you, unless one is born again, he cannot see the kingdom of God." Nicodemus said to him, "How can a man be born when he is old? Can he enter a second time into his mother's womb and be born?" Jesus answered, "Truly, truly, I say to you, unless one is born of water and the Spirit, he cannot enter the kingdom of God. That which is born of the flesh is flesh, and that which is born of the Spirit is spirit. Do not marvel that I said to you,
'You must be born again.'"
John 3:3–7

If you want to finish strong then this chapter's suggestion is an imperative and nonnegotiable. The rest are either gleaned from foolish mistakes made by me or made by others, or they are from solid teaching that God has provided to me from godly teachers. In most cases, I have not tried to identify the sources.

Begin at the Beginning

We begin with the most obvious and most important priority. You must be born again. You must have a start or a beginning in order to finish. Faith is absolutely necessary to finish strong. The writer of the book of Hebrews reminds us that ". . . without faith, it is impossible to please him (God). . . ." The motivation for everything we do begins inside with the new heart and new faith God gives us at the moment of spiritual birth.

When I first came to faith in Christ, I did not appreciate or understand this. My thinking was improper. I thought my Christianity was simply an addition to the education and experiences that I had received at the Naval Academy, in the Navy, and at Harvard—addendums, so to speak, to the truths I had already learned. I felt like Christianity was a turbocharger added to an already well-oiled engine. That was an arrogant and mistaken belief on my part.

I discovered, as I became familiar with God's Word, that my engine had not been retrofitted or overhauled; it had been replaced with a new one at my new birth! My Christian heart was now a new heart, not a supercharged, rebuilt one—completely new! I soon discovered that my brain needed a transformation and renewal as well—if you will, a spiritual lobotomy. In short, my thinking and beliefs needed reloading to a new hard drive. All this was part of my new birth.

Without faith, it is not only impossible to please God, but it is also impossible to have a godly hope. Peter tells us that our faith has been given to us by God and as a result of that, God "has caused us to be born again to a living hope through the resurrection of Jesus Christ from the dead" (1 Peter 1:3). Without hope, very little is possible except existence. Finishing strongly is impossible without hope.

If, while you are reading this, you feel a tug from God that you should finish strong, and yet you have never been born again, then rest assured that you did not pick up this book by accident. The tug you feel is the Spirit of God speaking to your soul. Do not ignore Him! Turn to Appendix 1 and carefully read it. Take it to heart. Talk to someone you know who has a strong faith in Christ and settle the matter now. To make things very clear, it was Jesus—not me—who told Nicodemus that it was necessary to be born again. If that applied to Nicodemus, a senior mature Jewish leader, then it also applies to all of us.

So then, my prayer for you is this:

> May God give you wisdom to see that a new birth is the indispensable beginning of spiritual life. May He show you that, apart from this starting point, there can be no finish. May God bless you with this beginning, so that you will be able to finish strong.

3

◇◇◇◇◇◇◇◇◇◇◇◇

Know
the Goal

*Indeed, I count everything as loss because of the surpassing
worth of knowing Christ Jesus my Lord. For his sake I have
suffered the loss of all things and count them as rubbish,
in order that I may gain Christ.*
Philippians 3:8

You cannot finish strongly unless you know what the end goal is. All of life is important—the start, the middle, and the finish. The start is new birth in Christ. That is clear. But the middle and finish goals may be a little fuzzy and murky to many of us because of what we have been taught in our upbringing, in our education, our work, and the teaching we have received at church. This suggestion deals with this two-part question: "What is the goal of a strong finish and how does one accomplish that goal?"

Doing the Right Things Well

Let me explain it this way. In business we say, "It is not just doing things well that determines a successful business; it is doing the right things well!" In simple terms, you cannot hit "the Target" if you do not know what the target is! Alice, in Alice in Wonderland, was informed of this by the Cheshire cat:

> ALICE: Would you tell me, please, which way I ought to go from here?
> THE CHESHIRE CAT: That depends a good deal on where you want to get to.
> ALICE: I don't much care where.
> THE CHESHIRE CAT: Then it doesn't much matter which way you go.
> Alice: . . .So long as I get somewhere.

THE CHESHIRE CAT: Oh, you're sure to do that, if only you walk long enough.

We can do the same thing that Alice did—wander aimlessly or strive for the wrong things while never really discovering what the "One" "Right" thing is!

Perhaps you have seen the movie "City Slickers." In it, Mitch, the unhappy city slicker (played by Billy Crystal) is looking for meaning in his life. That is why he heads off to spend time at a dude ranch. At the ranch he encounters the crusty, gnarly Curly (played by Jack Palance). No one could have played Curly better. Curly is a real-life cowboy who seems to know just what he wants and how to get it. Mitch asks Curly for assistance on life's meaning. Here's the instruction Curley gives to Mitch:

> CURLY: Do you know what the secret of life is? [Curly holds up one finger] This. [He motions for Mitch to look at his one finger.]
> MITCH: Your finger? [Mitch asks with great puzzlement.]
> CURLY: One thing. Just one thing. You stick to that, and the rest don't mean [expletive].
> MITCH: But what is the "one thing"?
> CURLY: [Smiles a smile only Jack Palance can smile.] That's what you have to find out.

Curly reveals to Mitch the emptiness that the culture we live in surrounds us with—a high-sounding platitude that reeks of supposed wisdom, and yet devoid of any actionable substance. Mitch was no better off for it afterward, and neither will we be.

John Piper, however, comes at the issue biblically and sub-stantively. He states the goal in simple and easily understand-able terms.

God is most glorified in us when we are most satisfied in Him.

Did you get that? What is our objective in simple terms?

It is to maximize the glory that we can generate for
God with our lives.

How do we do that? We do that by becoming persons who are satisfied in Jesus, and in Him alone! Notice carefully that the key action verb here is "becoming"! We don't strive to be liked and admired by everybody—a church, a pastor, or even our wives. We may be liked, but that is not our goal. We don't try to give more than anybody else, even though we may give generously! We don't have to work ourselves to the bone, although we may be productive and industrious.

Becoming a person satisfied in Christ and Him alone is the target. "Becoming" is the key word. Have we ever considered just "becoming"? If we are born again, Christ has made us something different. We already have become something different, whether we know it or not. But have we begun to pray and strive to become a person who could be fulfilled if the only friend we had in the world was Jesus, and it was He and we against the world? "God will be most glorified in me (insert your own name here) when I have learned to be most satisfied in Him and Him alone."

You may have any number of objections to that goal. What about actions such as giving, working, helping others, etc.? Those are good things, aren't they? Answer, "Yes." But they are not the ultimate goals, nor are they the basis of our acceptance by God.

Tadpoles and Frogs

Let me explain how works fit in here. Let's use animal examples. What do tadpoles do when they are transformed into frogs—i.e., when they become frogs? They cease swimming constantly and become world-class jumpers with entirely new appetites. What do caterpillars do when they become butterflies? They are transformed into world-class fliers, with entirely new horizons for their hunger and new activities for their energy. Why do transformed tadpoles jump and transformed caterpillars fly? Because they have become new creations!

The same should be true of genuine Christians when we have been transformed into new creations. Our energies, our actions, and our appetites have completely revised purposes. The question is this: Have we recognized that? Or are we butterflies who are not flying but still crawling around on the ground being attacked by all the evils that once haunted us, when God has granted us the privilege to fly? Have we allowed God to engineer the transforming of our minds into living sacrifices?

Living sacrifices eventually become satisfied in God and Him alone. As new creations, we should have new identities, new appetites, and new powers granted us by our Transformer—God! Works are not the goal; however, they should be the natural outgrowth of who we have become. The more we become transformed, the more our works become the loving, normal, and plentiful evidence of the change that has been wrought in us.

Think about this with me. What did the New Testament converts accomplish? What works did they do?

There were few rich people, and fewer still high-ranking politicians, and yet they changed the world! Why? Because God transformed their lives.

How did they give? Even though they were poor, they gave sacrificially. Why? Because God renewed their minds about what was important.

How did they help each other? They shared all they had unselfishly! Why? Because they had an abundance? No! They did so because they trusted God to meet their needs.

How did they live? They lived changed lives. Why? Because they became so in love with Christ that they developed a satisfaction with Christ and Him alone.

And who got the glory? They certainly did not. We do not know most of their names, and they got no glory from us or any other generation. But God got glory and His Kingdom grew and those worshipping the true God grew in number.

Our goal is to maximize the glory that we can generate for God with our lives. That is what the New Testament church did, and the same should be true of us! We do that by becoming what God intended.

4

Run Your Race

Therefore, since we are surrounded by so great a cloud of witnesses, let us also lay aside every weight, and sin which clings so closely, and let us run with endurance the race that is set before us.
Hebrews 12:1

God is so wise! He is the author of diversity, even though we think we just discovered it in America in the twenty-first century. He created us all as different creatures. Those differences are what makes the church rich with talent, wisdom, gifts, and challenges.

I have been a jock, an aviator, a businessman, a Fortune 1000 executive, a business owner, a board member, a trustee, a seminary professor, a pastor, a husband, a father, and, if you were to ask my enemies, any number of other titles and epithets. However, that has been the race that God has set before me. But it's not your race. So don't try to run it! You are not meant to run it. As the writer of Hebrews says, we are to run the specific race set before us, not anyone else's race.

We Are Uniquely Created

God has uniquely created each of us, with a specific set of gifts, talents, skills, and passions. The race set before us is unique to us and no one else. I love the fact that God uses the word *race* to describe our life's journey. A race has a beginning and an end, and it requires God's gracious gifts and our effort to complete it. A race is not a nap, a sojourn, a hobby, a sideline, an idle pastime, or a vacation. It is a contest. A race is meant to be run competitively and seriously. The objective of the race is to give it your best with a view to the finish line and winning. But you may not always win every preliminary race.

Our daughter was a competitive swimmer from the age of six years. I can still remember watching her tiny, wet feet taking her to the starting blocks at what seemed like a huge pool for a six-year-old. The beauty of swimming competitively was this: each swimmer could feel successful even if he or she didn't win the event. How could they do that? Obviously, every competitor was vying to win the race and equally clear was the fact that only one swimmer could win. But each swimmer also was timed, and each swimmer had a time that was his or her previous "best time." If a swimmer improved upon the "best time," the event was a success—a confidence builder.

Our daughter's coach was a great coach, and he kept all of his swimmers focused on their previous "best time." Why did he do that? He did it because he wanted his swimmers to concentrate on improvement over time. So even if his swimmers did not win the race, if they had a new "best time," he and all his swimmers considered that a positive step toward an ultimate goal. As a result, his swimmers could leave a meet as "winners" if they established a new "best time." Over the course of a season, his swimmers improved, and, as they aged, they became more confident. His teams won championships year after year, and he developed each swimmer to his or her full potential.

The same is true in the spiritual realm with our transcendent race. The race is ours. It is serious and important to run it faithfully, but it is not to be compared or set alongside anyone else's! It is not a competition! We do not have to beat anyone. The right question is this: "Are we improving spiritually, setting new 'best times' from day to day as we live?" That is the test. And, just like in swimming, we will not establish new "best times" in every race. Some days may be complete busts. That is the nature of real life! The key question for each of us is this: "Will we continue to run faithfully in the next day's race?"

Some of us will stay working at our trade or occupation until God takes us home. Others will be retired by the system that we work under, and be required to seek out a new way of running the race. It may be volunteer work, a completely new career direction, or devoting serious attention to a family need such as caring for an ailing parent or a disabled child. The concept of retirement or cessation from work does not exist in the biblical record. So, the idea of quitting work and entering into an existence of self-indulgence and constantly seeking pleasure through leisure activities is antithetical to any biblical principle that I can discern. However, the concept of slowing down, changing direction, and seeking God's glory in a different avenue is very real. The race may be new and frightening, but the reward will be worth it. If we want to finish strong, then we will run our race and no one else's.

Remember, the one thing we all share together is that we are called to finish strong. Since the race is ours, and ours alone, everyone's finish will look a little different. That is as it should be. However, each of us can share the joy of knowing that a strong finish brings glory to the God who has loved us.

5

◇◇◇◇◇◇◇◇◇◇◇◇

Be Satisfied
with Progress

*Not that I have already obtained this or am already perfect, but
I press on to make it my own, because Christ Jesus has made me
his own. Brothers, I do not consider that I have made it my own.
But one thing I do: forgetting what lies behind and straining
forward to what lies ahead, I press on toward the goal for the
prize of the upward call of God in Christ Jesus.*
Philippians 3:12–14

Progress, not perfection, is all that we can expect this side of heaven. To expect perfection is to misunderstand the depth of the sin that indwells each of us. Real life involves success and failure. Three steps forward and two steps back happen regularly. The key is to build upon the successes and to limit the failures, being sure to learn from them.

What's Under the Surface?

My own life journey may be unique in this regard, but my pastoral counseling tells me that we all experience the following discoveries if, and only if, we are serious about our faith. The deeper I get into the Word and the more thoughtful my walk, the more God makes me aware of the deep-seated hidden sins within me. Oftentimes, the image that He shows me of myself is anything but flattering. Let me give you an example.

Let's say I have just finished numerous hours of study of a Bible passage, put my thoughts on paper cogently, and then presented those ideas to my church in a manner that I perceived was just right. What am I feeling when I finish teaching that lesson?

I'll tell you what I am feeling: Pride, entitlement, arrogance.

"I" just did a good thing. I'm feeling very bright. "I" just hit a home run with that presentation!

In addition, I'm feeling deserving of accolades. Someone should recognize my wisdom and skill.

The one letter word "I" dominates my psyche. There is no

recognition from me that God has supplied my understanding, no thankfulness for His guidance, no humility asking myself, "Did I learn and apply the lesson myself?"

There is no outward move to pray for my listeners that they may hear what God has for them and apply it for His glory.

And I have not yet asked myself, "What was my motive?"

The picture that God shows me of myself is of a self-absorbed, ungrateful, arrogant, prideful, improperly motivated pastor.

From the eye gauge of my church members, I may appear to them as nothing but good. Yet, in reality, I am merely dressed in "filthy rags"! What do I do when God shows me this picture of myself and my sin?

Depravity
◇◇◇◇◇◇◇◇◇◇◇◇◇◇◇◇◇

If I am thinking right, I thank God for showing me the depth of my depravity, I ask for forgiveness, and I step up to the plate again and get ready for the next week, humbled and prayerful. My study will be different next week, even though no one else may notice the difference. I will be more careful to ask, "Have I learned and applied the lesson first to myself?" I will be more careful to search my motives and ask myself, "Do I expect something from this as a payment or reward?"

I cannot expect to correct everything that is amiss in my soul all at once. I could not handle the load, even with God's help. Nevertheless, little by little, God removes the dross from my impure heart. God knows the pace of change I can endure, and He has said He wants to make us mature. I more fully understand why David says, "Search me, O God, and know my heart! Try me and know my thoughts" (Psalm 139:23). I need God's accountability on my soul. Over time, I am convinced, God does make a difference inside us.

You may be a perfectionist. I am married to one! Perfectionism is a most fertile ground for the attacks of the evil one. He comes at you in your imperfection and says, "If you were really a good Christian, you wouldn't struggle with _____ (you fill in the blank). No really mature believer is still schlepping around with that problem. You can't possibly finish strong!" If you are vulnerable at that moment, He has you in the palm of His hand. You may become discouraged, disheartened, disarmed and ineffective, and out of the Kingdom battle for a while. Yet there is no need for falling for Satan's lies. There has only been one perfect person, who had a perfect day, and it was not you or I.

If we are honest with ourselves, and ask ourselves, "When was the last time we had a perfect day?" we know the answer. The answer is "*Never!*" Jill Briscoe once said, "We have to make a decision to live in our knowings and not our feelings." If we are going to finish strong, living in our knowledge and not our feelings is a key ingredient. We will never be perfect in this life. Hear that, say that, and believe that. If you cannot overcome your perfectionism on your own, get help—a friend, a counselor, or a fellow rehabilitated perfectionist.

If you want to finish strong, learn how to be satisfied with progress, not perfection.

6

◇◇◇◇◇◇◇◇◇◇◇

Focus on What You Can Become

Brothers, I do not consider that I have made it my own. But one thing I do: forgetting what lies behind and straining forward to what lies ahead, I press on toward the goal for the prize of the upward call of God in Christ Jesus.
Philippians 3:13,14

When I ask men, "What have you done in the past?" I usually get answers in one of two possible extremes. They either answer with the incredibly wretched things they have done in past, for which they often have guilt, or they answer with what they consider are the incredibly righteous things they have done, for which they project a measure of pride. Of course, there are some who answer with elements of both these extremes, and still others who answer in the middle. An undue and improper focus on past sins (and the guilt sin generates) or past righteousness (and the pride it may generate) can lead to a poor finish.

The Guilt Trap

Guilt from past sins can be like a parasite. Parasites live off the lifeblood of a host. They can cause disease, sap energy, stymie growth, and, in extreme cases, cause death. They come in all sizes, from sub-microscopic to visible to the naked eye, and they can live both inside us and outside. The solution for getting rid of parasites is to separate them from their host by removing them or exterminating them.

Guilt, too, comes in all sizes and infects us, sometimes on the inside and often outwardly. False guilt also saps our energy, stymies our growth, damages the benefits of God's grace, and can make us useless in our Christian walk. Guilt, like parasites, can be frightening. The fear can paralyze us and leave us ineffective.

While we were in Africa teaching at a seminary, my wife became intensely ill one night. Her physician examined her and had a blood sample taken to a medical lab for analysis. The next morning, after getting the results of lab tests and the physician's diagnosis, I reported the results to my wife:

"I have good news and bad news. Which do you want first?"

"Give me the bad news first" she replied.

"The bad news is you have a fish tapeworm." My wife's jaw dropped, her eyes expanded to the size of small saucers, and I could read the fear on her face. She pictured a six-foot tape worm she had seen in a high school biology text and assumed the worst! To say she was paralyzed and frightened would be an understatement. At that moment, she thought her life had ended. She was paralyzed and unable to think or act.

I then told her the good news:

"Take this one small pill the doctor prescribed, and that will take care of the tapeworm."

She took the pill, and the next morning she was cured. The parasite was eliminated and paralyzing fear was gone as well. She was back to normal, in physical terms.

Spiritual guilt and the fear it may engender also has a cure—an eliminator. The gift of forgiveness earned by Christ's finished work is available to every sinner and it works better than the pill my wife took.

Paul was a sinner who suffered from guilt. The Bible says that at the point of his conversion it "goaded" him, it poked him, it nudged him and said, "Pay attention to me!" Paul considered himself a blasphemer, persecutor, an insolent opponent of God, and the foremost sinner of all. He killed Christians, imprisoned and tortured others, ripped families apart, and blasphemed Christ. Paul never forgot nor made little of his past wretchedness. Yet, when he became a Christian, he was convinced that Jesus had forgiven *all* his past sins, his current sins, and even his future ones. The real guilt that he had for the real sins he had committed was exterminated by Christ's atoning sacrifice on the cross. That extermination of his real guilt set Paul free to minister and to become the most effective ambassador for Christ in the Gentile world.

Just imagine what might have happened for Paul if he had not believed God, and he had allowed his past sins to dominate his life and eliminate the ministry that God had for him! The key to his becoming what God wanted him to become began with believing that he could lay aside all the baggage of his sin, and begin as a new creation. Paul knew there was a penalty for his personal sins. As God began to instruct him, he began to understand that the penalty for his sins was just as Moses had written in Genesis: it was death—Paul's death! Paul saw there was no way for him to make himself right again with God, but God shared with him that Jesus suffered his sin penalty for him, and now he was permanently free to live a forgiven life. Guilt feelings might come to him with each sin he committed; however, he knew that Christ's blood covered all infractions. His guilt need not remain and paralyze him. Jesus had freed him from the penalty of sin, provided the power to resist current sin, and one day in the life to come, it would perfect him from ever sinning again.

Act on the Truth

If we are to finish strong, we must understand the same truth, believe it, and act upon it. Our baggage is different than Paul's, our sins are unique to us, but the laying aside of our past sin and guilt is the same. We, like Paul and every genuine Christian, have become new creations. God has good works laid up for each one of us to do. Obsessing over God-forgiven sin is a sign of unbelief.

The opposite of that extreme may be seen in an individual who takes such pride in his past successes, righteous acts, and current goodness that he forgets what a wise elder once said to a group of Christian leaders: "Today's success and righteousness is no guarantee of tomorrow's faithfulness."

To my chagrin, I was eyewitness to just such a failure, not long after I heard that comment. A very successful lawyer in our congregation—a former chairman of our elder council, a seemingly godly father, teacher, leader and son of a seminary professor—left his wife and children and cohabited with his secretary. He was raised in a Christian household, professed faith at an early age, and depended on his past goodness for his strength. He had not sewn his wild oats as a young man, and he took pride in that record. He leaned on his past goodness to carry him through. It was a lethal recipe for a poor finish. His righteous endurance ran out. No one knows exactly what motivated him to this failure, but his past track record of righteousness was no guarantee of his finishing strong.

A Lifelong Process

Focusing on "becoming" the "new creation" that God intends is a lifelong process. Becoming mature in Christ is not a sprint but a marathon, the length of which is the years that God gives us.

What we are meant to become is distinctive for each of us, just as the race before us is unique. Paul gives us four clues in the Philippians 3:13 passage above that can help us in our pursuit of our "becoming" the men that God has called us to be. This instruction has both defensive and offensive elements.

Paul said first that he was not doing his work alone. He was not on his own, and neither are we. God had indwelt him and indwells us with His Spirit, the very Spirit of God. We have access to that Spirit as Paul did. The Spirit acts both *defensively* for us, protecting us from things we cannot see (and sometimes even from ourselves), and *offensively*, giving us the power to proceed and the motive to mature.

Secondly, we are to strain forward. This is an offensive act. Straining forward implies that our becoming will require energy—and not just mild or moderate energy, but strenuous exertion! This is not merely a casual effort. This will be hard work. To expect to become what God intends us to become and, at the same time, believe that it will be a cake walk is unrealistic. It will be a joyful straining, but straining, nonetheless.

Thirdly, we are to press on. This pressing on implies stamina in the process.

Fourthly, as Paul says, we are to keep in mind the goal for which we are striving. This is strategic offensive work that we are doing. It is not mindless activity or busywork, but purposeful endeavoring.

Therefore, past sins need not keep us from becoming what God intends us to become, and past success will not guarantee us a strong finish.

7

◇◇◇◇◇◇◇◇◇◇◇◇

Become More Dependent on God

Yet he [Abraham] did not waver through unbelief regarding the promise of God, but was strengthened in his faith and gave glory to God, being fully persuaded that God had power to do what he had promised. This is why "it was credited to him as righteousness."
Romans 4:20–22 (NIV)

The key words I want you to focus on in the Romans passage here are how he "was strengthened in his faith." Paul is speaking of Abraham. He "was strengthened"! He did not do the strengthening himself. Someone outside of him did it. God did it!

It Seemed Impossible
◇◇◇◇◇◇◇◇◇◇◇◇◇◇◇◇◇◇◇◇◇◇◇◇◇◇◇◇◇◇◇◇◇◇◇◇

Abraham understood that he and Sarah were beyond child-bearing age. He struggled with the irrationality of God's promise that he and Sarah could have a child. But he did not waver. Why? Not because he tried harder, or worked harder, or became more confident in himself. He did so because he had learned to depend on God to do that which he could not do on his own—strengthen his faith. Notice Paul says that this strengthening of his faith resulted in Abraham "being fully persuaded"! If you want to finish strong, you must learn how to depend on God to do those things which you cannot do yourself. Abraham was weak by nature; however, God was in the "faith-strengthening-business." For our good, He is still in that business!

Here's another illustration: The Bible says that we are to speak the truth with love and gentleness. I can speak the truth naturally and easily. That has never been a problem for me. However, to speak the truth with "love and gentleness" is beyond my human capabilities. My human expressions of love and gentleness fall far short of what God calls for. For many years, I read the Scripture and obeyed the first part of God's instructions to speak the truth but ignored the latter instruction, never realizing I was falling short. That's the best I could do, I reasoned, and I assumed that God would understand.

Then, one day, God made it clear that I could not pick and choose which parts of Scripture I liked—based on what I could master on my own—and ignore the other parts. I could not choose "to speak the truth" and blithely disregard the instruction to do so with "love and gentleness." To be obedient, I needed to do both. I was almost paralyzed because I knew my own capabilities and I knew I lacked the sensitivity to be loving and gentle. I don't like being dependent, but, in order to become what God intended me to become, I had to give up my independence and become dependent on Him.

I had to pray, "God, I know You want me to speak the truth with love and gentleness. I'm okay with the truth part, but the love and gentleness parts are a different matter. If You want me to do that, You are going to have to help me and put the words in my mouth, and the compassion in my voice, because I don't have either! To be honest with You, God, I am petrified to take on this task, but I will take the risk! Help me!" That is what Abraham did. He trusted God to be true to His Word, and God was. God also was true to me. He gave me the words I needed—words that I would have never thought of on my own. And He can and will do the same for you, if you ask Him.

Rugged Independence?

Where does this idea of independence come from? Some of it comes naturally from our sinful nature, and some of it comes from American culture. John Wayne movies were (and still are) favorites of mine. They depict a lone hero, independent, an icon of rugged individualism and needing no one else. The characters he plays are always able to correct wrongs single-handedly with power and might that come from a strong will, a determination that is steely, skill that is uncanny, and insight that borders on supernatural. He needs no one, he is self-sufficient, he always knows exactly what to do, and it always works out well. Maybe right, maybe wrong, but never in doubt! Does that really portray your life and mine? Only in our dreams!

Many of the character qualities that Wayne portrayed were biblically commendable—his courage, his taking responsibility, his understanding that there is good and evil in the world, and that evil needs to be opposed. But often the one thing missing is the reality of his dependence. Who gave him his physical prowess, who enabled his skill, and who sustained his life and gave him a mind that surpassed the mind of his adversaries? Who gave him life, and breath, and sustenance? God did! He could have done nothing if God had not enabled him to do so. For everything that he was and did, God had to supply the wherewithal to make it so. The point is simple: Most John Wayne movies depict an independence that is as unrealistic as a Walt Disney cartoon. Yet, I and others have been impacted by this illusion of independence.

Paul was as dependent on God for his mission as were Moses, David, Elijah, and every other godly biblical character. Even Jesus said, "I do nothing on my own authority but speak just as the Father taught me. And he who sent me is with me. He has not left me alone, for I always do the things that are pleasing to him." (John 8:28-29). Jesus was dependent on His Father, and so are we.

Becoming dependent is not mystical or mushy. It is a necessity for maturing. If we want to finish strong, we must learn to be dependent on God and give up the illusion of independence that we may be embracing.

It will require that we learn to attempt things in faith that we may know we are incapable of doing on our own. It means risking failure and depending on God for results, not on ourselves. That is scary, especially the first time. Every time we do it and trust God for the result, it gets a little easier and less scary. However, there is no guarantee that God will always answer as we ask or that things will come out as we had planned and hoped. This is not because God is untrustworthy or that He is not listening to us. It is because what we ask for and what we may be expecting are not God's best for us and not best for the Kingdom. Our motives are not always pure, and our solutions may not always be the proper ones.

However, I can offer this assurance: When God receives a godly request given with a pure motive, and we experience His intervention to supply us with what we cannot do for ourselves, our faith is strengthened. Our hope is fortified and the next time we ask, it becomes a delight to wait on God's answer. Regularly and routinely depending on God means that we have settled the matter for ourselves—God is trustworthy. We also have learned that, apart from God, we can do no good thing. Becoming dependent and letting go of our independence is not an easy task for some readers! It goes against much of what we have been taught as men, it is countercultural, and it is initially frightening! But, let me be clear, it is worth the risk!

8

Take Responsibility

What then shall we say to these things? If God is for us,
who can be against us?
Romans 8:31

God created man first and gave him clear instructions. He was to be fruitful, increase in number, fill the earth, care for it, and rule it as God's representative—in the way that God would rule.

Then God gave His command to Adam concerning the trees: "You may surely eat of every tree of the garden, but of the tree of the knowledge of good and evil you shall not eat, for in the day that you eat of it you shall surely die" (Gen. 2:16–17). This command was not onerous or harsh. God gave an amazing abundance of other plants, fruits, nuts, and trees for Adam to eat from, and He pronounced all of that "very good."

Deception

Eve then was deceived by Satan, and she ate of that tree of knowledge of good and evil and gave some of its fruit to Adam. Yet, God principally held Adam responsible, and not Eve. Later—in the New Testament—Adam is also the one held responsible for the first sin, not Eve. It is clear, then, to any rational reader of Genesis 1–3, that God intends the man to be ultimately responsible for the affairs of the family. God addresses Adam, not Eve; God commands Adam, not Eve; and, even though Eve is deceived first, Adam is ultimately held responsible for the first sin.

If you are to finish strong, one of the things you must recognize as a man is that God intends for you to be ultimately responsible for what goes on in your family. Whether that family is a single-person family, a single-parent family, a family of fifteen children, or a multigenerational household, God intends the man of the house to be ultimately responsible. That does not relieve a wife of her own responsibility, or any child or additional family members of their personal responsibility, but the man of the house is nevertheless the one that God looks to as the leader who is accountable.

There is a saying often used by pastors in the south, and maybe it is used all across the nation, that goes like this: "If Momma ain't happy, ain't nobody happy!" It implies that if the family is to function well, then the ultimate test and measure will be if the woman of the house is satisfied. "Momma" is held up as the ultimate judge of what should and should not go on in a household. We all understand what the little adage means because even Solomon, the writer of Proverbs, says that a quarrelsome wife is like a constantly dripping roof in a rainstorm, which makes no one happy, including "Momma." Is the adage true? Biblically, is Momma really the chief judge of what should be and what should not be? Is she the chief arbiter of right and wrong in the family? Of course not!

Men Must Be Responsible

Therefore, every time I hear that saying, I cringe! The biblical untruth in it and the poor theology it subtly encourages are detrimental to the mature growth of a wife, the family, the children, and especially harmful for men! The saying totally ignores God's purpose that men be responsible, and, instead, encourages men to be jesters and stooges, responding with haste to every whim and desire of their wives with due speed to head off any unhappiness. Good luck with that!

On the contrary, our charge, under God, is to love our wives as Christ loved the church. The only charge I see equal to that is the reciprocal charge to wives to honor and respect their husbands as the church is supposed to love Christ. Both charges are humanly impossible to fulfill, and neither charge is to primarily make the other "happy." Both are far more purposeful than that, and also much harder to accomplish. May we dispense with the homey nonsense and focus on the godly wisdom given to us!

I love how John Piper puts it in his book, *This Momentary Marriage*. He says that when God knocks on the door of a home and the wife or child of the house answers the door, Christ is going to say, "Is the man of the house here?" Piper states clearly what the maxim gets wrong: "Husbands are responsible!" God is the only judge to be reckoned with in the management of our households.

We need to get this theology straight if we are to finish strong. We need to take our rightful responsibility for our household and recognize that God is the only judge that matters.

9

◇◇◇◇◇◇◇◇◇◇◇◇

Think in Biblical Terms

*For whatever was written in former days was written for
our instruction, that through endurance and through the
encouragement of the Scriptures we might have hope.*
Romans 15:4

Thinking biblically implies knowledge. Paul praises God for "the riches of [his] wisdom and knowledge" in Romans 11. Therefore, if you are to think biblically, you must know your Bible. You ought to know more than "Jesus loves me," and the dozen or so other most-common verses and shibboleths. You should immerse yourself in the rich treasury of human history that the Old Testament provides; you should savor the deep teachings of Paul's church letters; and you should pray and ask God to imprint on you the truths that Jesus taught so ably about the practical issues of life. If you have never read the entire Bible and attempted to apply its teaching to your everyday life, then you are deceived in telling yourself you are thinking biblically.

Centering on God's Word
◇◇

Thinking biblically means more than just casually saying that you are in your Bible. The Bible must be in you. Its teaching should exude from the pores of your everyday existence into the life you are leading in a pagan culture. Your speech should be sprinkled with biblical thoughts and ideas, so much so that you cannot help but radiate the warmth and life-giving richness of the Bible's wisdom. Your ethics will then be governed by what you know to be true. To finish strong means that your life has been built on the solid biblical beliefs of the Kingdom.

Are you willing to study your Bible? I am not talking about a five-minute tapioca or pablum devotional in the morning with a dandy-sounding little ditty at the end. I am not talking about any effort that culminates only in a check in the box for the day that says, "My Bible Study Duty is Done." Instead, what is needed is an intentional, serious, commitment to thought and study with the hope that God will transform your heart and thinking.

Paul instructed Timothy in this way: "Do your best to present yourself to God as one approved, a worker who has no need to be ashamed, rightly handling the word of truth" (2 Tim. 2:15). Paul implied that there is a right way to handle God's Word and a wrong way. To learn the right way is work, approved work, necessary work. But it is work nonetheless. One of the elements of that work is for you to search for and understand the context of each passage. In real estate, the key phrase is "Location! Location! Location!" In Bible study, a key phrase is "Context! Context! Context!" Get the context wrong and often the interpretation and application will also be wrong.

A Text out of Context is a Pretext

An article in *World Magazine* illustrated what can happen if context is not considered. The article was about Christians who had lost their faith after being raised in Christian homes, and sometimes employed in Christian ministry. By implication, these people were presented as well-taught and knowledgeable. One individual example cited by the author said he had read Jesus' words in the Sermon on the Mount, "You therefore must be perfect, as your heavenly Father is perfect." He took those words out of their context, both as they were presented in the sermon and in the message of the entire Bible, and believed that he was being called to live a perfect, sinless life. Of course, he experienced failure after failure, until he became so disillusioned that he abandoned his faith.

The context of Jesus' words was completely missed. The perfection needed for this young man (and for all of us) can only come from the substitution of Jesus' righteousness, not our own. None of us can possibly ever be perfect even for one day or one hour. Because he did not consider context, this man could not think biblically, and he threw himself a serious curve ball.

Thinking biblically was constantly on Paul's mind. He told the church in Rome that their spiritual act of worship was to be transformed by the renewal of their minds. Biblical thinking was what Paul wanted for the Roman church. How does that happen? It happens by asking God for a biblical hunger, for biblical thinking, and a biblical mindset! There are not three easy steps to accomplish this. There are not any shortcuts. There are, however, the glorious, gold-filled pages of wisdom that await the soul who pledges to take this life's journey—a journey whose end is a transformed mind and a changed life, leading to a strong finish.

10

◇◇◇◇◇◇◇◇◇◇◇◇

Willingly Die to Self

Though I myself have reason for confidence in the flesh also. . . .But whatever gain I had, I counted as loss for the sake of Christ. . . . For his sake I . . . count them as rubbish in order that I may gain Christ . . .becoming like him in his death.
Philippians 3:4–10

Dying to self is giving up the things that mean the most to us apart from God—the hopes and dreams that drive us, temporarily satisfy us, shelter us, and sometimes delude us into believing we are protecting ourselves. This dying to self never ends; it simply begins, and then bores deeper and deeper into who we are in the flesh.

What—You Won't Fire an Adulterer?

What I remember about the day I began to die to self are these words: "You can't fire David!" Those words came out of my boss' mouth as he leaned over the small round table we sat at in his penthouse office. I'll never forget those words.

I was responsible for 900 employees (90 percent of them were women) at four locations. One of my division presidents had had an affair with one of his employees. Word was that they had met and consummated the affair at the office.

After getting all the facts and talking with the offending president, the facts were confirmed, and they were clear. I decided that the president had to go. How could I run a business where I asked husbands to send their wives to a workplace where the husbands had every right to be worried that the boss might be hitting on their wives? It seemed like a no-brainer to me!

Off I went to the CEO's top-floor office to get the final okay, expecting the conversation to be short and sweet. How wrong I was!

I presented the evidence. The case was solid—open and

shut. There was no debate about the facts. When I finished, I heard these words: "You can't fire David!" It took me a few seconds to recover my equilibrium. I hadn't expected a debate or a refusal.

"Why?" I asked.

"Well," the CEO said, "I look at every female employee who walks in the door as a possible bed partner, and we can't fire someone for doing what I do regularly."

I won't bore you with the whole debate. The gist of it went like this.

- The Bible—"Boot that out," he said. "It has no relevance here at work."
- Adultery will pollute the culture—"Well, David had hundreds of wives, and concubines, didn't he? So, what's wrong with me pursuing other women?"
- So, what about the husbands' concerns?—"That's their problem, not ours!"
- It's just not right—"Says who? I don't care what the Bible says!"
- Sexual harassment—well it never even came up. The "me too" movement was way after that time.

After about forty-five minutes of heated discussion, I was spent and stunned. I had not come prepared for a debate. I assumed the issue was so intuitively clear, and the solution so obvious, that this would be a succinct briefing with an equally brief approval.

Eyeball to eyeball, I said, "You're the boss. I must do what you say. However, I'm not sure I can manage this way, and I'm not sure I want to learn how!"

I left the office with my mind spinning. The ethics of the place I was working at were not what I assumed that they were. How had I missed such an obvious and glaring moral standard of behavior? Now I had a huge dilemma. Could I stay where I was and enjoy the security that my job gave me or did I have to leave because I could not do business God's way?

I had joined this company in order to make a lot of money and advance quickly, and so I had. The corporation had already given me restricted stock grants that amounted to several millions of dollars. All I had to do was acquiesce to the boss' instruction and stay in place! I had grown up poor, had always wanted to be financially secure, and this job was giving me that opportunity. Could I manufacture a way to compromise what I knew to be the right thing to do, in order to maintain the lifelong financial security that I so earnestly wanted? The answer did not come easily!

But God had other opportunities in mind for me. I had no idea what those were at the time. Eight years earlier, I had become a Christian and God was now feeding me biblical truth through a fire hose at our local church. I took that truth to heart! I asked myself, "Could I honor God and manage in an environment that is not just secular and pagan, but also hostile to biblical principles?"

Doing the Right Thing—Even if it Hurts

To find an answer, I studied Daniel who worked for a pagan. He managed to maintain his integrity and also to flourish. Nehemiah did the same. I asked for advice from godly men. A classmate from the Academy, who was much more politically astute than I was, tried to help me. However, he couldn't grasp the biblical arguments that the Spirit of God kept bringing before me. I couldn't figure out how to walk the tightrope upon which God had placed me. Leaving meant dying to my most treasured hopes and dreams, and this was the hard lesson that God was teaching me. I was learning what it meant to die to self.

With tears in my eyes and no idea what was next, I decided I had to leave. Maybe someone else could've managed the ambiguity, but I couldn't. I wasn't as mature as Daniel or Nehemiah! I walked away from the millions and the security I had always sought. My boss never understood why I left! At the time, I didn't either. But with hindsight, I realize that the decision was part of running the race and finishing strong. My endurance would have been depleted in that environment, my righteousness tested beyond my abilities, and my Christian growth stymied.

That was over three decades ago. I can see now what I couldn't see then: God wanted me to grow up, to trust Him for security and not the company. I had to begin the process of dying to self and, to finish strong, I had let go of my deepest desires for security. What a great temptation it is to view our companies, our bosses, or our retirement plans as our security.

What treasured hopes and dreams do you need to give up and entrust to God? To finish strong and endure to the end, we must die to ourselves.

11

✧✧✧✧✧✧✧✧✧✧✧

Commit to Finishing Strong

But as for me and my house, we will serve the LORD.
Joshua 24:15

This may sound a bit simplistic, but sometimes it's the simple things that give us the most trouble, and not the complex ones that we don't understand. We must commit ourselves, under God and with His help, to finishing strong. That is step one in godly endurance.

Exemplary Models

Isn't commitment what Abram demonstrated (Gen. 12:1) when he left his country, his people, his family, and his position in society to go to a land he knew nothing about?

Isn't commitment what Jacob exhibited (Gen. 35:2) when he returned from exile and removed all the foreign gods in his entourage and recommitted to the covenant?

Isn't commitment what Joshua attested (Josh. 24:14–15) after the conquest when he publicly stated, "But as for me and my household, we will serve the LORD"?

Isn't commitment what Ruth declared (Ruth 1:16) when she told Naomi, "Your people will be my people and your God my God"?

Isn't commitment what Elijah demanded when he asked the people (1 Kings 18:21) to declare their allegiance to Yahweh or Baal, ". . . .if the LORD is God, follow him; but if Baal is, follow him"?

Isn't commitment what Shadrach, Meshach, and Abednego proved when they replied to Nebuchadnezzar in these words: "We do not need to defend ourselves before you in this matter.

If we are thrown into the blazing furnace, the God we serve is able to save us from it, and he will rescue us from your hand, O king. But even if he does not, we want you to know, O king, that we will not serve your gods or worship the image of gold you have set up"? (Dan. 3: 17–19).

Isn't commitment what Peter and the other apostles displayed when they followed Jesus, every one of them, to their deaths or to exile?

Isn't commitment what we all ought to demonstrate? What I am saying is this: There ought to be a time in every genuine believer's development as a disciple, that we promise:

> God, I am yours. I am all in. Above everything else in life, I want You to know that I want to be all Yours, I want to live well, and I want to finish strong! In order to do this, I will need Your help, God. Today, I am asking for it. During the times when my passion for finishing strong wanes, I need Your encouragement and inspiration. During my times of confusion with what direction to take, help me to grow in wisdom and knowledge. During my times of fatigue and discouragement, strengthen my will to fulfill this commitment.
> In Christ's name I ask it.
> Amen.

12

◇◇◇◇◇◇◇◇◇◇◇◇◇

Develop a Mind for the Things of God

But he [Jesus] turned and said to Peter, "Get behind me, Satan! You are a hindrance to me. For you are not setting your mind on the things of God, but on the things of man."
Matthew 16:23

In the twenty-first century, the written word has been displaced by media. We live in a day of images, sounds, and emotions: television, movies, videos, and YouTube dominate the contemporary scene. Social media is more important than the *New York Times*, and our local newspapers are going out of business right and left. Politics, medicine, education, and entertainment dominate our energies and time with thirty-second snippets or sound bites. These are man-centered things. As Jesus admonished Peter in Matthew 16 for his man-centered thinking, it is easy for us to understand Peter's problem, to have his mind set on the things of man. In Peter's day, and in every era since, the things of our human existence clutter our daily lives and fill our calendars. Today, more than ever, we are bombarded with messages, most of which have their origin in humanism, not Christianity.

Your Mind Matters
◇◇◇◇◇◇◇◇◇◇◇◇◇◇◇◇◇◇◇◇◇◇◇◇◇◇◇◇◇

God chose to reveal Himself in a written language, not pictures, not sounds, not musical notes, not math, and very seldom in pithy snippets. If we are to develop a mind for God, we must be people who read and can appreciate the nuances of the various forms of text that the Bible feeds us: narrative, poetry, history, prophecy, personal letters, and more. We also must be people who are willing to dig and search for complex ideas and solutions that take longer than a thirty-minute television show to completely flesh out.

The Bible is God's way of revealing Himself to us. It shows us His character, His heart, His actions, His people, how His creation works best, and what makes it malfunction. It is a book of enigmas. Some of it is easy to read, some of it is hard to read; some of it is easy to understand, some of it is hard to understand; yet God has promised us that, by believing in Christ, we may comprehend and understand it. The world says, "Seeing is believing." God says, "By believing, you will be able to see." That partly explains why God's Word is such an enigma. To an unbeliever, much of the Bible seems outdated, irrelevant, nonsensical, and impractical. It is only after a person believes, that God provides a proper lens through which we can clearly see the message He intends.

Even in the churches, non-written means of conveying truth have begun to dominate—videos, dance sequences, slides, PowerPoint presentations, and computer graphics just to mention some. This is not to imply that all of this is evil. It is not. In and of themselves, none of these things is evil. However, in many cases, they are simply unable to communicate complex ideas and concepts as effectively as the written, spoken, and preached Word.

Dedicated Discipline

If you want to finish strong, you must develop an exercise regimen for your mind that is rigorous. Notice that Jesus said to Peter that he should set his mind on the things of God. Setting one's mind is an exercise, a willful routine that trains the mind to function in a certain way, to respond to stimuli in a certain way, and to retain learning material in a certain way.

It is only by setting one's mind rightly that we will be able to process complex and nuanced arguments, and then translate those arguments into biblical practical applications. Paul tells Timothy to "Do your best to present yourself to God as one approved, a worker who has no need to be ashamed, rightly handling the word of truth" (2 Tim. 2:15). This implies that there is a right way to handle the Scripture and a wrong way.

Don't "Share Your Ignorance"

◇◇

One famous pastor described much of today's Bible study as "S.Y.I." Bible study. By "S.Y.I." he meant, "Share Your Ignorance." He characterized this improper study as events that begin by reading a passage and then immediately going to the question, "What does this mean to you?" This kind of study fails to wrestle with careful observation, and never deals with the important question "What did the original writer intend this to communicate to the original readers?" Improper study also leads to silliness, nonsense, and misapplication. This is an erroneous way of handling the Bible's message.

Howard Hendricks outlines a solid method of Bible study in his material, *Living by The Book*. In it, he outlines a careful process of observation, followed by interpretation, and then application. He emphasizes the importance of understanding what the original writer meant to say to the original readers before we ever begin to try to apply a passage to our lives. Like sensible and effective physical exercise regimens, good Bible study regimens produce superior biblical results. That is what Paul meant to say to Timothy and to us.

The mind is not a muscle, but it needs to be exercised just as muscles do. It can also be developed and strengthened just as muscles can. If we are to finish strong, we need to develop our minds into well-toned, mature muscles for God.

13

◇◇◇◇◇◇◇◇◇◇◇◇

Cultivate God-Pleasing Appetites and Passions

Therefore, preparing your minds for action, and being sober-minded, set your hope fully on the grace that will be brought to you at the revelation of Jesus Christ. As obedient children, do not be conformed to the passions of your former ignorance.
1 Peter 1:13–14

Developing God-pleasing appetites and passions is closely related to the developing of one's mind; but differs in the methods that we use to achieve maturity. Passions and appetites are associated with emotions, feelings, and enthusiasm, rather than the mind. The mind is like a muscle, and it is best trained and developed by apt, regular exercise. Not so with all passions and appetites; since they are often fleshly lusts and glandular impulses, these drives are often unhelpfully encouraged by regular bodily exercise. Instead, exercise may cause one to feel a glandular rush of momentary ecstasy that passions sometimes carry with them that encourages us to more sin, not less. Therefore, something very different is needed.

When Running Away Is the Right Thing

In simple terms, two things are needed: you should "flee" from certain things and "pursue" certain other things. Jesus dealt with this issue when he told His disciples, "and do not set your heart on what you will eat or drink. . . . But seek his kingdom and these things will be given to you as well" (Luke 12:29,31, NIV).

Jesus was saying that you should not passionately devote yourself to certain things but, more simply, flee from them. He pointed out the examples of eating and drinking because they were common appetites and easy to understand, but He implied other passions and appetites as well when He encouraged them to seek other things—Kingdom aims. Flee from some things, and, at the same time, pursue other godly things. These are two completely different tactics which face in opposite directions—*flee* and *pursue*. Why?

Because some things are transient and, in light of eternity, unimportant. *Do not* let lesser urges captivate you! *Flee* from them. What kind of things? Things that are fleeting, less significant, and sometimes distracting from the best things in the scheme of eternity. These are not mere physical appetites and passions, like eating and drinking, but any hunger that sidetracks.

However, Jesus did not leave His disciples with just an instruction on *what not to do!* He also instructed them on *what to do!* They should pursue certain other things. What kind of things? Things that have eternal significance and that are lasting. He gave a positive *Do this!* and a negative *Do not do this!* The *Do not* instruction is a defensive strategy to *flee*, and the *Do this* is an offensive strategy to *pursue*.

Self-Discipline

So how does one properly develop one's passions and appetites? The answer lies in discipline—self-discipline. Paul says it often in his letters in this way. We need to learn how to say no to certain things and to say yes to certain other things.

Jim Elliot, the missionary to the Quichua Indians of the Ecuadorian jungle, who was brutally murdered in the course of his ministry, lived out this *fleeing* and *pursuing* strategy while he was a student at Wheaton College. While at Wheaton, he met a young lady named Elisabeth Howard. We know her as Elisabeth Elliot.

Elisabeth was smitten with Jim and, at the end of a school year, she asked Jim to sign his picture in her yearbook. He gladly complied with a personal inscription, signing his name to his photo and, below it, penning the words "2 Timothy 2:4." Elizabeth rushed back to her dorm room to look up the Scripture that Jim had cited. Scrambling to see what endearing and romantic words he had referenced, Elisabeth turned to 2 Timothy 2:3-4, which says, "Share in suffering as a good soldier of Christ Jesus. No soldier gets entangled in civilian pursuits, since his aim is to please the one who enlisted him."

Jim doused her romantic hopes, but he was modeling Christ's instruction. He was saying that his passion and affection for Elisabeth was eclipsed by his pursuit of pleasing his Savior. Fleeing from his attraction to Elisabeth was important to the Kingdom and to Jim's maturity. Pursuing his missionary Kingdom work at that time was his highest priority. Jim fled from a good thing to gain a greater thing. It is no wonder that later Elliot would say, "He is no fool who gives up what he cannot keep to gain what he cannot lose." Eventually, God would show Himself as true to His Word, "But seek first the kingdom of God and his righteousness, and all these things will be added to you" (Matt. 6:33). Years later, Jim and Elisabeth were granted the privilege of marriage to each other.

Fleeing and Pursuing

The desire to know which items are on the *flee* list and which are on the *pursue* list can only come from a heart that is filled with the truth and is deeply rooted in a desire to please Christ. This is a lifelong endeavor. Out of love for what He has done for us, not Pharisaism or compulsion, we ask ourselves, "What passions and appetites will He be pleased with?" One side effect of this pursuit is that those passions and appetites that will please Jesus are also the ones that will bring us to maturity and fullness of life. Therefore, fleeing and pursuing should not be considered a burden, but a blessing.

All of this fleeing and pursuing is countercultural today. We live in a culture that believes that the way to happiness is to pursue any passion or appetite that brings us pleasure, even if that delight is momentary. "Pursue it with gusto," our people in our society say and, by implication, they suggest it will be satisfying. This is exactly the same lying that Satan used to lure Eve and Adam into sin in the Garden. Satan led Eve to believe that the fruit from the Tree of the Knowledge of

ENDURE ⫸⫸⫸⫸⫸⫸⫸⫸⫸⫸⫸⫸⫸⫸⫸⫸⫸⫸⫸⫸⫸⫸⫸⫸⫸⫸⫸

Good and Evil was pleasing to the eye, good tasting, and would make her wise like God. She said yes when she should have said no. Adam was no better. Satan's lies provided pleasure for a moment, but that moment didn't last long. As soon as God showed up to meet with His two special creations, the jig was up. Their pleasure was displaced by sudden urges to hide from God, to cover up their nakedness, and to manufacture excuses for their disobedient behavior. Guilt, separation from God and repercussions followed, and life would never be perfect again for Adam and Eve. Their appetite for sinful things brought an end to Paradise.

As human beings made in the image of God, we are not meant to be slaves to our fleshly passions and appetites. One of the things that separate us from the animal kingdom is that we are able and expected, as we mature, to keep our unhealthy passions and appetites in check, by developing healthy, godly appetites. To finish strong, we need to pursue the wondrous joy of holy, healthy appetites and passions, while we flee from unhealthy ones.

14

◇◇◇◇◇◇◇◇◇◇◇◇

Develop a "Habit Pattern" Mindset

*Show yourself in all respects to be a model of good works, and
in your teaching show integrity, dignity, and sound speech that
cannot be condemned, so that an opponent may be put to shame,
having nothing evil to say about us.*
Titus 2:7–8

Activities repeated often enough to cement them into our brains are habits. Habits accumulate randomly or by training. Habits begin with a problem to be solved or a routine event that needs to be completed. We find a solution that works, is satisfying, and we stick to it—thus a habit pattern is born. Some habits are routine and of little spiritual consequence: brushing one's teeth; combing one's hair; etc. Habits of spiritual consequence are a different matter. They entail motivations, cravings, desires for rewards, character, ethics, moral behavior, and thoughts. For Christians, our motivation for godly habit patterns should be love for Jesus. Biblical authority guides us, not our intellect or emotions. Our rewards are inward jewels—the peace that comes from being in intimate fellowship with the Father and a desire to hear the words "Well done, good and faithful servant" (Matt. 25:23). The question for all of us is this: "How healthy are my character and spiritual habits?"

Your Life Depends on Right Habits

Let me illustrate this principle of just how important habit patterns can be from experience on the flight deck of a combat aircraft carrier. When flying combat missions from the Gulf of Tonkin, the heat on the flight deck was often over 100 degrees. Add to that the fact that the deck was a tar-black color and that 20–40 jet tailpipes were all spewing superheated blasts at the same time as engines started and aircraft were launched.

The point is simple. The flight was hot, very hot, very humid, smelling of jet fuel—and it was dangerous.

Our flight gear included a flight suit, a G-suit, a survival vest that weighed fifteen pounds and covered our entire torso, Nomex gloves, a flight helmet with visor, and high-top boots—not what you want to wear in stifling heat! Before every flight, the aircraft had to be inspected. A combat pre-flight inspection was tedious and time consuming: nose, refueling probe, port wings ailerons, flaps, check every bomb on the port wing for proper hanging and fusing (we carried twenty-eight of them), integrity of the fuselage, tail, and tail hook, and then repeat everything on the starboard side. By the time you climbed into your ejection seat and strapped in, perspiration had seeped through your under-clothes and flight suit, and a torrent of sweat was dripping down your face.

We were taught to develop a correct "habit pattern" for every preflight inspection and mission. Do the right things. Never take a shortcut. Do the right things every time. Make the right things your normal "habit pattern." If you developed this "habit pattern" as your routine, your chances of survival were better.

However, because of the heat and the tedious, repetitive nature of the tasks, there was always a constant temptation to take shortcuts—things like this: assuming the bombs were properly fused; taking off your gloves to cool your hands; removing your helmet to feel a breeze; not strapping yourself into the ejection seat because it only added to body tempera-ture; or eliminating tedious parts of the preflight inspection that seemed like no-brainers.

It Didn't Have to End This Way

One night, one of our carrier pilots and his aircraft was diverted to Da Nang airfield for the night. Da Nang was in South Viet Nam. He spent a joyous night in the Da Nang O'Club Bar, an amenity that aircraft carriers do not have. Awakening the next morning with a hangover, he got into his jet and hastily took off. It was a routine flight back to the carrier, with no combat mission at all—no bullets to dodge, no missiles to avoid. In his haste and lack of good habit patterns, he did not strap himself onto his ejection seat, and he left his Nomex gloves off to stay cool. He had not developed good habit patterns. His aircraft had an engine fire on takeoff. His aircraft had a zero, zero ejection seat, meaning the pilot could eject at ground level and zero speed and still live through the ejection. He should have been safe, even though the aircraft would be lost. The pilot ejected from the aircraft, the seat deployed as it was designed to, the chute deployed, and the seat drifted to the ground safely. The pilot, however, was separated from the seat since he was not strapped in, his hands were burned so he could not take hold of anything to help himself, and he was propelled like a stone to a peak and then splatted on the runway to his death. His lack of a good habit pattern cost him his life.

Habit patterns are equally important for us as Christians if we are to finish strong. Let me illustrate with some questions for each of us to wrestle with.

- When we are faced with a dilemma, like making a decision, where do we go for advice and counsel?
- Is our motivation always to make our decisions in the best way for the Kingdom and our Savior, or are other sources of rewards more important to us?
- Are we moved more by what other people will think or feel than what God approves?
- Do we even think of God when we are faced with a dilemma?
- When faced with the prospect of lying or telling the truth, do we always tell the truth?
- Are we missing the peace that passes all understanding that comes with knowing our response is always to tell the truth?
- When tempted to cheat, do we ever consider it a legitimate option?

- If no one is looking, do we believe we are safe to do whatever we can get away with?

I am sure there are more questions we can ask ourselves and I hope we will, however, I hope you get the idea. Have you begun the process of developing habit patterns so that you can answer the above questions with godly answers, a clear conscience, with honesty, and certainty? We do this so that our joy may be complete! What joy? The joy of knowing we have made every effort to be in complete fellowship with Christ.

The sooner you begin this process of making habit patterns a part of your life, the sooner you will begin to see growth and contentment. Great peace comes from knowing what you are doing is what you have been doing and what you will continue doing—no concealment, no guile, no manipulation. Peace with God. That peace was purchased by Christ, and is now enjoyed by you because you have rightly answered the question, "Who is the authority in your life?"

15

◇◇◇◇◇◇◇◇◇◇◇◇

Know Your Greatest Enemy: Enemy #1

Now Joseph was well-built and handsome, and after some time his master's wife cast her eyes upon Joseph and said, "Sleep with me." But he refused. "Look," he said to his master's wife, "with me here, my master does not concern himself with anything in his house, and he has entrusted everything he owns to my care. No one in this house is greater than I am. He has withheld nothing from me except you, because you are his wife. So how could I do such a great evil and sin against God?"
Genesis 39:6–9

Mike Stokke, Men's Ministry Pastor at Parkside Church, came to me with an idea and asked, "I am thinking about having a class for men on *holiness*. It will consist of only three sessions. What do you think?" I answered rapidly, "I think that is the dumbest idea I have ever heard of! You will get the small group of men who consider themselves holy and the rest will take a pass! Let's do something else!"

Sexual Purity

Mike then clarified what he meant: "No, you don't understand. I want to speak directly and frankly to men about sexual purity and what that means in our culture today. I counsel men over and over again, and they don't even seem to know the basics. We need this!"

"That's different," I replied.

We changed the name of the sessions. I can't remember what the new name was, but we planned three sessions and we wanted to speak bluntly about sexual topics that seem to escape discussion in polite Christian circles—pornography, masturbation, the way God made men for sex, etc. We began the first night with 150 men. We freely admitted our weaknesses and did not try to present a "holier than thou" attitude.

Most of these types of classes start with a certain number of attendees and, as the sessions go on, the audience tends to decrease. However, these sessions were different. The second session's attendance was almost 200 men, and the third grew as well. Consequently, we decided to expand the class to six sessions. Each gathering continued to grow. Our men were hungry to hear and learn from other men what we, as men, struggle with, and how we can deal with these battles in a biblical and godly manner.

What does this have to do with "Know your greatest enemy"? Sexual sin is arguably the main enemy that attacks men and lures them into finishing poorly. We are vulnerable, we are enticeable, and sometimes we are even willing. In church, we often avoid this reality and speak boldly and less than truthfully about our weakness with this temptation. Our lack of candor and honesty with one another as men does not serve the Kingdom well.

The other two enemies are money and power. They will be dealt with in the next chapter. Money, sex, and power have long been the traps that have ensnared men for centuries. The rich young ruler and the Sadducees were seduced by money. David and Solomon were lured by sex. Power corrupted Saul and Gideon in their later years. Men today have the same three enemies.

As a combat aviator, I needed to know, understand, and prepare for my enemy. The tactical enemy we prepared for in Viet Nam was different than the strategic enemies we prepared for on the world stage. Knowing my enemy's capabilities and my own capabilities and limitations was basic. It is also basic for every man today!

Enemy # 1: Sexual Immorality

The sessions we had at Parkside were over thirty years ago. The Internet was in its infancy. Online pornography was not as developed as it is today.

We did a survey of those two hundred men who attended the sessions and asked for anonymous answers to a myriad of questions. We found that over 80 percent of the attendees had had some level of involvement with pornography in the past year and several were having online affairs as they attended the sessions. One attendee was simultaneously conducting online affairs with five different women. Why do I highlight these findings? I do so to remind us that, "but for the grace of God, there go I"! We are all vulnerable, and the temptations of sexual sin are alive and well, even in the best of churches. If you are a male, then sexual sin is crouching at the door. Its desire is for you, but you must rule over it (see Gen. 4:7).

My Own Struggle, Too

How can men help other men? Let me give you one example. Several years ago, my wife and I had serious marital problems. The details of those problems are not important here, but what is important is that I was cut off from normal sexual relations for a period of almost a year, and the temptations of masturbation and pornography were very real. I wrestled alone with the temptation, thinking I was the only pervert who could possibly be so corrupt!

By God's grace, I was given a book *Triumph Born of Tragedy* written by a friend, Andre Thornton. Andre was a young, outstanding professional baseball player whose wife and daughter were tragically killed in an auto accident on the Pennsylvania Turnpike. Andre was left as a committed Christian, a handsome young athlete spending many nights in hotel rooms away from home, with fawning female fans at every stop. The temptations of sexual sin for professional athletes are legion and they were real for Andre. In providence, God gave Andre a mentor, J. Vernon McGee. J. Vernon advised Andre to pray and ask God to take away his sexual desire until God provided a legitimate, proper outlet for it for him.

Ask God to remove your sexual desire? My sexual desire? That seemed crazy at first! What if God never restored what I once had? I realized I could never have thought of such a solution in a million years, and yet that solution was just what I needed. In tears, I asked God to do that which I thought was crazy, and, to my surprise, God honored the request. I cannot say I never grappled with the thoughts again, but the scrapes were few and far between. In the throes of temptation, I learned to re-pray the same prayer, and each time God ended the conflict.

Andre was honest with his struggle. His honesty helped me. I hope my honesty may help you! One of the Evil One's strategies against men is to suggest to us that what we are thinking and feeling is unique to us. He wants us to believe that something must be wrong with us, and we are the only deviants who could imagine such horrible images and activities. His intent is to isolate us and send us into our quarantined closets to struggle alone. Many of our thoughts, especially when we are alone, are not honorable or godly! They arise from our depraved, sinful nature which is common to all men. Notice I said to "all men." We are not alone in this combat. Other men fight the same battles! Until we cross life's finish line, our struggle with sexual sin will continue.

Guiding Principles

These biblical truths are worthy of writing down and memorizing as helps in our battle with sexual sin. These are not original with me.

- After we come to faith in Christ, sin no longer reigns in us, but it remains.
- Jesus freed us from the penalty of past sin.
- Jesus provides us with the power to resist current sin.
- Jesus will perfect us one day in heaven from the presence of sin.

Many of the chapters in this book will be useful in any man's struggle against the enemy of sexual sin. Here are a few points and suggestions on how they might help with the sexual enemy.

- *Thinking biblically*—reminds us to live by what we know and not by what we feel. Sexual sin normally arises from intense feelings and urges.
- *Becoming dependent on God*—reminds us that we are never alone in this combat. God has supplied us with His Spirit to help us when we are weak, if we will lean on Him.
- *Cultivating God-pleasing appetites and passions*—reminds us to be diligent and disciplined in what we allow into our eyes, ears, and lives. We constantly have choices to make. Those choices will continue until God takes us home.
- *Developing habit patterns that are healthy*—reminds us that routines can be useful for righteousness. Daniel prayed every day at three specific times. That habit kept God in his mind all during the workday in a pagan land. Daniel's example prompts us to ask ourselves, "How is my prayer life?"

As you read these chapters, consider seriously how they may affect your thinking about sex, and then apply them to your everyday life. Sexual sin is a major enemy for every man, and it comes in many forms. That is why there are entire books written solely on the subject. Know your enemy and know yourself. Be honest about where your vulnerabilities lie.

16

◇◇◇◇◇◇◇◇◇◇◇◇

Know Your Enemies #2 and #3

But godliness with contentment is great gain, for we brought nothing into the world, and we cannot take anything out of the world. But if we have food and clothing, with these we will be content. But those who desire to be rich fall into temptation, into a snare, into many senseless and harmful desires that plunge people into ruin and destruction. For the love of money is a root of all kinds of evils. It is through this craving that some have wandered away from the faith and pierced themselves with many pangs.
1 Timothy 6:6–10

Money and power are so closely related to each other that I want to deal with them at the same time as complementary enemies. Money can buy power, and power can enable the amassing of money. It is more accurate and precise to say that the "love of money" and the "love of power" are the enemies, because money and power alone are simply tools which may be used for good or ill. It is when the lure of either one of these surpasses one's love of God and becomes the driving motive in a man's life that they behave as enemies. However, each of these enemies is an imposter. They promise happiness, satisfaction, security, pleasure, the absence of pain, and joy, but what they promise they cannot deliver. What they do produce is emptiness!

Love of Money and Love of Power

Two billionaires, John D. Rockefeller and Ted Turner, illustrate the emptiness of money and power apart from God. In the early 1900s, John D. Rockefeller was a billionaire when billionaires were unheard of. Many today consider him the richest man ever in the modern industrial era. His corporation was broken into thirty-four different companies and his net worth at the time was 3 percent of the US GDP. In today's dollars, that would be about $700 billion. One day, a reporter asked Rockefeller, "How much money is enough?" He answered the reporter, "Just a little more." No matter how much there is, or how little, if the love of money has taken root as one's primary goal and motivation, then there is never enough! "Just a little more," will always be tomorrow's hurdle. The love of money is never satisfying! The allure of the enemy, "love of money," is an illusion.

We, as men, should be able to see this "just a little more" in ourselves. If you were a car enthusiast as a teenager, you were probably delighted with a solid, cool, used car to drive to school. As you aged, however, that car was replaced with a newer one that was a step above that high school vehicle. Today, you probably drive a much nicer set of wheels than either of those two, and when you see your dream car pass you on the highway, the "just a little more" gremlin comes out in you. "Man, I wish I could have that one. Maybe next year!"

If you were not a car enthusiast, you can substitute any number of other things that grab your attention: a bigger, more powerful computer; a nicer home in a nicer neighborhood; your first RV or a fancier one; your dream boat; a gold-plated motorcycle like Clint Eastwood's; the next educational degree; the award or medal just ahead of the one you have; or a vintage shotgun instead of the one that Dad gave you.

Most of us have a soft spot or a weakness for something that can be purchased by money or power. I am not encouraging a lack of healthy ambition. On the contrary, I love it, but it needs to be properly grounded in the will of God.

Ted Turner, the second billionaire, even though not a believer, properly and profoundly identified power and money as the pretenders that they are. Ted was the founder of CNN, and WTBS, the first super TV station, which later became TBS. He, at one time, owned the Atlanta Braves, and is known as the largest private land holder in the USA and Argentina, with over 2 million acres and a net worth of $2.5 billion. To top all that, he donated one billion dollars to the UN for causes that he supported. In a television interview with Barbara Walters, Barbara asked Ted, "What is success?" In characteristic, direct fashion, Ted answered, "Success is an empty bag, but you don't know that until you get there." Here is a man who has both money and power, which he manages with worldly precision, and he recognizes that the achievement of all that he has accomplished is emptiness. Power and money's promise is just "air," a phantom, an empty bag, a mist that seems to be there one moment and then disappears the next.

However, the love of money and power is not confined to billionaires. Two men from more common means will illustrate how pernicious the love of money and power can be for all of us.

He Was an Unconverted Church Officer

Years ago, I had a Bible study for CEOs and prominent men of the community. One founding member of the study came in one morning as we opened in prayer and told the group he had something to share. He was a college professor, a married man, and was considered a solid Christian citizen. He addressed the whole group and, although he was not in tears, he was intensely serious. Here is what he said:

> I have been a participant of this group for seven years, and a member of my church for over twenty years. I have been a deacon and an elder. I considered myself a believer and a Christian. However, I have realized in the past few weeks in our study of the Bible that my real God has been my intellect and position as a professor. The power, feeling of competence and approval I received from my job, was what really drove me! When push came to shove, I worshipped my position and all that came with it. I loved hearing people say how smart I was and the influence that harvested. I was not a Christian until God spoke to me through His Word and confronted me with my idolatry. I have been chasing after the wind for all these years and I never realized it. This past week, I confessed my sin and became a believer for the first time.

The love of money does not have to come in billions of dollars nor is the love of power confined to prestigious multinational corporate executives or influential government positions. Here was a man who, on the outside, gave the appearance of being the genuine article, but on the inside had been worshipping his own idol. Yes, I said idol! Because, when we chase anything that is not God-centered, we are dogging an idol, no matter how good that thing is. There is nothing wrong with having a doctorate or any other career and enjoying the prestige and security that attends it—but when it becomes the obsession of one's life, carved out neatly and placed on the altar to be revered, that's another matter. Thankfully for my friend, he was listening to God speak, he was humble enough to be penitent, and God brought him into the fold.

The Power He Thought He Had. . .

The second man was molested sexually as a young boy. His parents knew of the molestation and did nothing about it. Therefore, deep inside, he convinced himself that no one could be trusted, not even God. Power and enough money to make him feel like he was in control of his life became his primary motivation. He went to church, told himself he was a Christian, but never could completely submit himself to anyone else, whether to man or God. His Christianity became more and more perfunctory. His relationships were shallow and his marriage crumbled under the weight of distrust. His need to always be the power person in any relationship cut him off from any source of constructive advice and counsel. He was never rich in the world's eyes nor was he powerful as a mover and shaker, but, in his own little world, he lived in a cocoon of fictional security. Power and the need for control emptied his life of everything meaningful.

This man listened to no one—not even to God. He was unable to receive any constructive discipline from God in any form, and believed that he had no need to repent of anything. He lived a life of darkness, fear, and increasing misery, because of an imagined invulnerability that was created by what he considered sufficient money and power.

Jesus deals with the love of money and power often, but none more directly than in the sermon on the mount. In Matthew 6:24, He says simply and clearly, "No one can serve two masters, for either he will hate the one and love the other, or he will be devoted to the one and despise the other. You cannot serve God and money." The last six words summarize Jesus' warning of the potential of money becoming a master rather than a servant.

Yet there is more here! Jesus was talking about more than money! A close examination of the Greek word translated by most of our modern versions of the Bible as "money" is actually a word that the King James Version translates "mammon." Mammon originally meant "anything in which a man puts his trust." The King James Version says "Ye cannot serve God and mammon."

In Old Testament times, people put their trust in their flocks and herds. These animals gave them a feeling of security. They could trust in their value. As time passed, flocks and herds became trade goods. They could be sold and replaced with gold, silver, and, later on, currency. That is why most modern translators use the word "money."

However, Jesus would have been aware of how this word "mammon" had been used in the past and selected it, just as He did every other word He spoke, precisely for what it had meant—"anything in which a man puts his trust." Therefore, those last six words can thus be translated in this way, "You cannot serve God and any other thing in which you put your trust." That includes the love of money and the love of power.

Chasing the Wind

Why is that so? Solomon answered that question with an answer that resembles Ted Turner's answer. Let's remember that during Solomon's reign, he was one of the wealthiest and most powerful men in the world. However, he says that his money—and what it could buy—along with all his accomplishments and power—was emptiness, vanity, a chasing after the wind, a gain of nothing!

And whatever my eyes desired I did not keep from them. I kept my heart from no pleasure, for my heart found pleasure in all my toil, and this was my reward for all my toil. Then I considered all that my hands had done and the toil I had expended in doing it, and behold, all was vanity and a striving after wind, and there was nothing to be gained under the sun.
(Eccl. 2:10,11)

As men, we are immersed in a culture that surrounds us with empty promises. A good financial planner will always ask his client, "How much do you think that you need to live on and retire with?" That question forces the client to deal with the trap that Rockefeller fell into—always desiring more! I am not your financial planner, but I will leave you with two questions.

- Have you asked yourself how much is enough?
- Have you asked God to search your heart for anything in which you put your trust besides Him?

17

◇◇◇◇◇◇◇◇◇◇◇◇

Heed the Bible's Warnings

I appeal to you therefore, brothers, by the mercies of God, to present your bodies as a living sacrifice, holy and acceptable to God, which is your spiritual worship. Do not be conformed to this world, but be transformed by the renewal of your mind, that by testing you may discern what is the will of God, what is good and acceptable and perfect.
Romans 12:1,2

Never Stop Renewing Your Mind

To finish strong means nurturing an attitude of constant learning, repenting, revising, and growing. Doctor Luke tells us that ". . . Jesus grew in wisdom and stature, and in favor with God and men" (Luke 2:52). The writer of Hebrews then tells us that "Although he was a son, he learned obedience through what he suffered" (Heb. 5:8). If Jesus grew from learning and continued to do so during His entire life—and learned even from His sufferings—so can we. Learning ought to be a lifelong pursuit and experience.

Never Assume That You Have Arrived

. . . you yourselves like living stones are being built up as a spiritual house, to be a holy priesthood, to offer spiritual sacrifices acceptable to God through Jesus Christ.
(1 Peter 2:5)

We will not arrive at full maturity this side of eternity. Each one of us should always be developing and growing. Our wills control our growth and development. In a negative sense, our wills are much like a rheostat. A dimmer switch on a dining room light fixture is a rheostat. You can turn it to "bright" or "dim" or anywhere in between. We control our wills in the same way. We can will ourselves to be fully available to God and to full obedience to His will. By the same logic, we can alternately choose to will ourselves to a minimal commitment to God and only token obedience to His will. The choice is ours. We control our own willful rheostats. We can lay open our wills to be fully available to "GROW AND CHANGE", or we can shut them down and post an internal sign with the words "OUT TO LUNCH—UNAVAILABLE."

If you think you have arrived and are perfected in your current condition, that is a definite sign that you are not. We have been set apart by Christ at our new birth and are now holy in God's sight because of Christ's work. While we are alive on this planet, we are being sanctified by God's Spirit and God's grace. That process is ongoing and never ending until death. We will be completely sanctified when we go to be with God in heaven. Until then, we have not completely arrived. Never assume you have arrived.

Never Forget Who You Are

> But you are a chosen race, a royal priesthood, a holy nation, a people for his own possession, that you may proclaim the excellencies of him who called you out of darkness into his marvelous light. Once you were not a people, but now you are God's people; once you had not received mercy, but now you have received mercy.
> (1 Peter 2:9–10)

Remembering our identity in Christ is paramount to remaining on a steady path to spiritual maturity. As believers, we are chosen people, members of the royal family, endowed with all the benefits of the universe. We must consider this and also remind ourselves that we received this identity because of the grace of God, not because of our merit or how special we are. We deserved punishment for our sin—but instead, God chose to make us His own.

Because of His grace and love, we now have the very Spirit of God within us, we can speak to the world's Creator one-to-one, and we will have His ear. With our Creator, nothing is impossible. Being forgiven and having our sin debt paid is only a small part of the identity that God bestows on us. To finish strong, we should remind ourselves of the identity we have been given.

Never Forget Who Is in Charge.

Be subject for the Lord's sake to every human institution, whether it be to the emperor as supreme, or to governors as sent by him to punish those who do evil and to praise those who do good.
(1 Peter 2:13–14)

As Americans, we love to think that we are in charge. We value our freedom and our independence. On a human level, those values are precious and can be virtuous. God grants all humans the right to freedom of choice, the ability to agree with God and obey Him or disagree with God and make our own rules. Independence is also a good character trait when applied to a young man or woman who has now matured enough to leave home and make a new home and start a new family.

Yet, each of these values, carried to the extreme, can be harmful to us. We are free, but as free people, we also all answer to a higher authority. We do so at home, at school, at work, in our communities, and—ultimately—to our Creator. To forget that, or never know it, is to be deluded into believing we are our own highest authority—our own god. Nothing could be further from the truth, and nothing could be more dangerous. We are created beings made in the image of God, and He is ultimately in charge. He is sovereign, omnipotent, all-wise, and omnipresent. And we are not.

Never Forget There Will Be a Judgment

> His master said to him, "Well done, good and faithful
> servant. You have been faithful over a little; I will set you
> over much. Enter into the joy of your master."
> (Matt. 25:21).

The most precious words we can ever hope to hear from God's lips are these: "Well done, good and faithful servant!" Those words tell us first that we belong to Him. We are His. Second, they remind us that He has purchased us, and we are His valued possessions. Third, they reveal to us that our service has been noticed and, not only noticed, but also accepted as good. Finally, we hear from God in heaven that we have been judged faithful.

The most frightening words were spoken by Jesus in Matthew 7:23: "And then will I declare to them, 'I never knew you; depart from me, you workers of lawlessness.'" One day we all will stand before our Creator and we will hear either, "Well done," or "Depart from me." If we are to finish strong, then we need to never forget that one day there will be a judgment.

Never Forget That God's Objective for Us Is Not Our Happiness, but Our Maturity

> In this you rejoice, though now for a little while, if
> necessary, you have been grieved by various trials, so
> that the tested genuineness of your faith—more precious
> than gold that perishes though it is tested by fire—may
> be found to result in praise and glory and honor at the
> revelation of Jesus Christ.
> (1 Peter 1:6-7)

Hedonism and humanism currently reign supreme in the contemporary culture of America. They are not only accepted, but they are also praised, and their influences have permeated the church. They were also rampant in the first-century church.

Hedonism says that the end of all being is the maximization of pleasure for mankind. Paul related this to Timothy in these words:

> But understand this, that in the last days there will come times of difficulty. For people will be lovers of self, lovers of money, proud, arrogant, abusive, disobedient to their parents, ungrateful, unholy, heartless, unappeasable, slanderous, without self-control, brutal, not loving good, treacherous, reckless, swollen with conceit, lovers of pleasure rather than lovers of God, having the appearance of godliness, but denying its power. Avoid such people. (2 Tim. 3:1-5).

These words were directed at folks with a "form of godliness," who were seeking pleasure in everything they did. These folks were Timothy's church members, not pagans. This was meant by Paul as a warning to Christians and teaching for godly leaders. This is a warning for all of us in the church today!

Humanism says that the end of all being is the happiness of man. "Seek whatever makes you happy," so the humanist says. "Seek it with all your energies and you will be satisfied and fulfilled." Yet our world is populated with sad, dejected, unsatisfied wanderers seeking contentment in every vice and virtue, and finding it in none. James writes that we are to, "Count it all joy, my brothers, when you meet trials of various kinds, for you know that the testing of your faith produces steadfastness. And let steadfastness have its full effect, that you may be perfect and complete, lacking in nothing" (James 1:2-4).

Trials are tests of our faith and, in the world's eyes, they do not produce happiness; rather, they produce anxiety, angst, and a desire to run away from them. But, for the genuine believer, trials produce maturity which, ultimately, produces lasting joy.

Joy is very different than mere happiness or momentary pleasure. Joy is a deep-seated, firm satisfaction and peace that all the important matters in one's life are settled and put to bed. Joy allows us to deal with hardship, suffering, pain, disease, and disappointment not with stoic disassociation but with calm confidence that God has the matter covered—even if we cannot see the covering. It is the knowledge that suffering may bring us closer to maturity which enables us to endure it with joy.

Even when some church communities adopt the "happiness of man" as their driving principle, we can know that joy comes from growing into maturity, not seeking to fulfill our every glandular fantasy. Happiness alone and pleasure alone are delusions of the real thing. The joy of the Lord is our strength. If we suffer from the delusions of hedonism or humanism, we will be discouraged by life, disillusioned about God, and fall short of our objective of finishing strong. Godly endurance is impossible if all we seek is a jolly good time!

Never Forget That Pride Is a Stalker of Us All

Pride goes before destruction, a haughty spirit before a fall. (Prov. 16:18)

A retired accountant friend of mine took a job as a choir director at a small church for a minimal salary. He was in his sweet spot! He was a gifted musician, a capable director, and he was thriving and satisfied in the position. He did not need the salary from the church to live comfortably as he began his work. The small salary was an insignificant issue for him as his retirement pay was sufficient. As I talked with him, there was an evident sense of contentment in his soul over the work that he was doing. He was singing and serving the King. What could be better than that?

As time went by, the church went through several cycles of salary increases for all the staff and none of these cycles seemed to make a dent in the joy that this fellow had in his job. One year, the church was in distressed financial straits and the increase they proposed to my friend was a pittance.

My friend's wife took great offense at the perceived "insult" the raise represented, and the specter of prideful sin began to creep into his thinking. His wife's consistent nagging convinced him that he had been disrespected. He began to think to himself, "I have done great work for them! I have provided them with service over and above what was called for! How dare they treat me so disrespectfully?" In anger he quit his job, the job he loved, over a salary dispute that virtually had no bearing at all on his quality of life. Pride polluted his judgment! He never completely recovered from that resignation.

No new position opened up at another church, even on a volunteer basis. He died wishing he had never let so trivial a matter cause him to leave his life's love of music performed for the King of kings! Pride got him and destroyed his loving service. Pride is "crouching at the door" of every believer who is trying to finish strong. If it can happen to this friend of mine, a committed believer, then it can happen to any of us.

Never Fall Prey to Sloth

The sluggard buries his hand in the dish; he is too lazy to bring it back to his mouth. The sluggard is wiser in his own eyes than seven men who answer discreetly. (Prov. 26:15–16, NIV)

Laziness is never acceptable in God's house, and yet every one of us hears the call of a well-deserved rest—and that rest can be extended; and then extended; and then extended again. The first rest is healthy; the extensions are not! One could argue that David was more vulnerable to Bathsheba, because he was slothful in his duties as king. If David was vulnerable, then so are we!

God is quite concerned with idleness and slothfulness. The old saying that "Idle hands are the devil's workshop" is borne out in Scripture. Sloth can lead to poverty, to shame for inattention to duty, to a ruined reputation, to ruined relationships, to discouragement, to disillusionment, and much more. Most important to enduring well is the fact that sloth is antithetical to many of the suggestions God gives us to help us finish strong.

Biblical study is hard work and you cannot do it idly. Learning self-discipline requires both mental and physical exertion, the opposite of rest and idleness. Growing and developing require energy and toil. And so it goes for almost every virtue that we need to finish strong. But we need to remember that God also gives us His Spirit. It is His Spirit that can give us energy when we think that we are spent. It is His Spirit that can encourage us to go on when we think we are exhausted. It is His Spirit that reminds us, "I know you can't do it, but with God all things are possible."

Adam was given work in the Garden before sin came into the world. That work was meant to be purposeful and meaningful service for his Creator. He was not to be idle and lazy! What a joy it must have been to work in a perfect garden, with no weeds, thistles, insects to destroy harvests, or disease to harm his crops. Adam was a regent for the Lord of lords, the ruler and caretaker for the only perfect patch of earth ever known.

We live on an earth that is far different from Eden, but our charge, as God's people, is the same as Adam's charge was: Rule and care for the earth and everything God has made, and do it in a fashion that will be honoring to its Creator. The church is now one of God's creations and it needs care and rule. God's people are His creation, and they need care and governance. None of this work that we have been blessed with can be done from a bed or the comfort of an easy chair. To stay in bed or remain in the recliner is to admit to no desire to finish strong. Sloth is the enemy of finishing strong and of righteous endurance. Be warned against it. Flee from it. But always remember to pursue the joy that comes from labor done for the King— and done in the way He desires.

Postscript

My hope is that these thoughts in this short book will be helpful in preventing another failure like Jesse's (mentioned in the Introduction) or a failure like that of many other Christian men. I pray that all genuine believers will be encouraged to become diligent students of the gospel and want to complete further study on their own.

These suggestions are designed to change the reader's thinking. Thinking drives behavior. Faulty thinking leads to faulty behaviors and, conversely, right thinking leads to godly and permanent changes in behavior. Theology consists of beliefs, and beliefs are the substance of our thinking. We all have a theology. Our individual theology is what we actually believe.

What we believe (think) is tested by the trials of life; the results of those trials become convictions; those convictions then become attitudes; and finally, those attitudes lead to changed behaviors. Here is a brief word depiction of what I just said.

Beliefs >> *Trials* >> *Convictions* >> *Attitudes* >> *Behaviors*

My behaviors in my life have not always been godly. In fact, often they have been quite sinful, and sometimes in the worst ways. I have attempted in this book to share my mistakes, so that you don't have to make the same ones that I have. I pray that the results of this sharing will be that you will experience a shorter path to maturity than I had.

Appendix 1

Understanding the Basics

The starting point for life with God is the Christian gospel. You can only finish strong if you've begun a new spiritual life by understanding, believing, and accepting the gospel as true. The gospel message can be described under four headings: *Creation*, *Fall*, *Redemption*, and *Grace*.

CREATION
◇◇◇◇◇◇◇◇◇◇◇◇◇◇◇◇◇◇◇◇◇◇

The gospel begins with God who is the Creator of all things. By His Word alone, the universe was created, including countless galaxies, solar systems, and planets. Chief among them was Earth, which contained a paradisiacal garden called Eden. In it, God placed His masterpiece of creation—man and woman whom He made in His image. They were created for the purpose of worshipping, loving, and serving God. Delighting in Him as their Creator, Father, King, and Treasure was designed to be their highest and most satisfying calling.

However, the magnificent beauty and perfect harmony of Eden was altered by a tragic fall from innocence and perfection.

FALL
◇◇◇◇◇◇◇◇◇◇◇◇◇◇

In addition to man and the material world, God had also created spiritual beings called angels. There was a rebellion among angels led by an angel named Lucifer, whom we know as Satan, whose desire was to usurp God's throne and overthrow His rule. Having failed to achieve his malevolent purpose in heaven, Satan took the form of a serpent and visited Eden. There, in Eden, he deceived Eve into believing that God was withholding the fruit of one particular tree because He didn't have Adam and Eve's best interest in mind. Subsequently, they disobeyed God and ate the forbidden fruit—Adam disobeying knowingly, and Eve being deceived. Their first sin spread like a contagious virus, instantly entering into their lives, affecting not only them but all humans after them and all of creation with them. Thereafter, sin, suffering, and pain have been mankind's legacy.

However, that was not the end of the history. God did not leave man in his fallen sinful condition but, instead, came to his rescue and recovery. We call that redemption—and redemption is entirely a work of God.

REDEMPTION
◇◇◇◇◇◇◇◇◇◇◇◇◇◇◇◇◇◇◇◇◇◇◇◇

Although God expelled Adam and Eve from Eden, He covered their sin (or atoned with or substituted) with the blood of sacrificial animals and promised to provide them with a permanent Redeemer from sin. One of their descendants would, one day, be born into the human family who would redeem sinners from the consequences of the sin introduced to mankind at the fall. Over the many centuries that followed, God's prophets foretold the arrival of this Redeemer who would be mankind's Savior.

In fact, the focus of the entire Bible points to this one Redeemer whose ultimate mission was "to seek and to save what was lost" (Luke 19:10, NIV). This promised Savior was Jesus who, 2,000 years ago, was born of a virgin, lived a sinless life, and died as a substitute and sacrifice for all sinners who would trust Him. In the greatest demonstration of divine mercy and grace the world has ever witnessed, an innocent Jesus died to rescue and recover guilty sinners. We say Jesus is our substitute. Taking our sins upon Himself, Jesus was punished by the Father for sinners like us. The innocent Jesus was punished for the guilty, in order to satisfy divine justice. However, three days after His crucifixion, as foretold by the prophets, Christ rose from the dead. In this act, God declared His victory over death, sin, and the grave. And forty days later, after repeatedly appearing to His followers, Jesus ascended to the Father in heaven where He now rules and reigns as the triumphant King, and intercedes on behalf of all believers. God accomplished all of this because He is gracious.

GRACE

Why did God do all this for rebellious people like Adam and Eve, and you and me? He did so because He is a God of grace. Grace means "unmerited favor." For any of us to be in a right relationship to God, God says we must be perfect. That means we must be sinless. None of us qualifies. None of us deserves to be in the presence of a holy God. We cannot earn our way to heaven or live a perfect life, so, as humans, we are in a hopeless condition. On our own we might as well give up and call it quits.

But John tells us the good news: "For God so loved the world, that he gave his only Son, that whoever believes in him should not perish but have eternal life" (John 3:16). That is God's grace. What we could not obtain on our own, God provided for us with the birth, life, death, resurrection, and reign of Jesus. The unmerited favor of God, God's grace, makes a way for human beings to have eternal life. What we couldn't obtain on our own, God, in His grace, has provided for us. We don't get what we deserve; we get what we could never earn. By God's grace, spiritual life is possible and a strong finish can now be in our sights!

WHAT SHOULD BE OUR RESPONSE TO GOD'S GRACE?

Our response to God's grace should be to believe. Believe the gospel, believe that God is who He says He is. Believe that

Jesus is who He said that He was. Jesus' disciples asked Him a question that is similar to our question above. Here is their question and Jesus' response as recorded in John's Gospel:

> Then they [Jesus' disciples] said to him, "What must we do, to be doing the works of God?" Jesus answered them, "This is the work of God, that you believe in him whom he has sent."
> (John 6:28–29)

Jesus' answer was simple: Believe in Jesus.

The real test is this: "Is this belief genuine?" Knowing the right answer and spouting it out at the right time is not what we mean by believing. Genuine belief involves a recognition of the following things at least.

- God is in charge, and I am not.
- I have sinned against God—the God who is holy.
- All of my sins are deserving of punishment.
- I repent of those sins and I want to turn completely away from them.
- I understand that Jesus died in my place for my sins to make me holy before God.
- I accept His sacrifice on my behalf.
- By His grace alone, I now belong to a new master, God.

If this commitment is real, many things will begin to change in your life. These are some concrete signs that this commitment is real and genuine.

- I will begin to have a desire to be in God's Word, the Bible. If we love someone, we want to communicate with that person. The Bible is God's way of communicating with us.
- I will develop a desire to be among God's people. This may be a completely new affection. Before we believed, we may have desired to be as far away from Christians as we could.

- The Spirit of God within a new believer will begin to make Himself evident. This will occur suddenly for some people or sometimes gradually, but a new, genuine believer should begin to feel uncomfortable with sinful things that once were easy to do and be around. That is the living Spirit of God communicating to the new believer's spirit. This action can be quenched for a time, but, if belief is real, the sense of conviction will return until it is acknowledged and acted upon.
- Affections and appetites will begin to change. Old ones that are sinful will wane, and new ones will begin to take their place.

If none of these things occurs, the commitment made was more than likely spurious and disingenuous. If this happens, the individual needs to go back to the starting point of Appendix 1—the Gospel. Something important is missing. Belief in Christ is not a little thing! It is a commitment of one's total self. Halfway measures will not suffice. Wholehearted repentance for sin is part of genuine faith in Jesus Christ. Genuine faith is what is necessary!

Appendix 2

Additional Resources

In the next pages is a list of books that may be useful for the reader who wants to do further investigation. I have arranged the books according to the chapters they may help illuminate.

Chapter 1. Take Your Finish Seriously

- Steve Farrar *Finishing Strong, Going the Distance for Your Family*
- Eric Metaxas *7 Men and the Secret of their Greatness*

Chapter 2. Be Born Again

- Chuck Colson *Born Again*
- C. S. Lewis *Mere Christianity*

Chapter 3. Know the Goal

- John Beckett *Loving Monday*
- Eric Metaxas *Bonhoeffer*

Chapter 4. Run Your Race

- Bob Richards *The Heart of a Champion*
- Eric Metaxas *Luther*

Chapter 5. Be Satisfied with Progress

- A. W. Tozer *The Knowledge of the Holy*
- Brother Lawrence *The Practice of the Presence of God*

Chapter 6. Focus on What You Can Become

- Bob George *Classic Christianity*
- Wayne A. Barber *Living Grace*

Chapter 7. Become More Dependent on God

- John Bunyan *Pilgrim's Progress in Today's English* (retold by James H. Thomas)
- George Muller *The Autobiography of George Muller*

Chapter 8. Take Responsibility

- John Piper *This Momentary Marriage*
- Alistair Begg *Lasting Love: How to Avoid Marital Failure*

Chapter 9. Think in Biblical Terms

- James Montgomery Boice *Whatever Happened to the Gospel of Grace?*
- David Wells *The Courage to be Protestant*

Chapter 10. Willingly Die to Self

- Dietrich Bonhoeffer *The Cost of Discipleship*
- A. W. Tozer *The Crucified Life*

Chapter 11. Commit to Finishing Strong!

- David McCullough *The Pioneers*
- David McCullough *John Adams*

Chapter 12. Develop a Mind for the Things of God

- James Montgomery Boice *Renewing Your Mind in a Mindless World*
- Neil Postman *Amusing Ourselves to Death*

Chapter 13. Cultivate God-Pleasing Appetites and Passions

- J. I. Packer *Knowing God*
- J. I. Packer *A Passion for Faithfulness*

Chapter 14. Develop a "Habit Pattern" Mindset

- Jerry Bridges *The Discipline of Grace*
- Jerry Bridges *The Practice of Godliness*

Chapter 15. Know Your Greatest Enemy

- Heath Lambert *Finally Free*
- Archibald D. Hart *The Sexual Man*

Chapter 16. Know Your Enemies Two and Three

- Randy Alcorn *Money, Possessions, and Eternity*
- Ron Blue *Mastering Money in Your Marriage*

Chapter 17. Biblical Warnings to Heed

- R. Albert Mohler *The Gathering Storm*
- Paris Reidhead *Ten Shekles and a Shirt* (A sermon available online in audio or PDF)

Study Guide

This study guide was put together to help you internalize the principles that are presented in *Endure: A Christian Man's Guide to Finishing Strong*. It begins with questions on the "Introduction" and covers all of the chapters in the book. As much as possible, the guide attempts to direct your mind and thoughts to the Scriptures where these ideas come from. To the best of my ability, I have attempted to make sure that the perspective of the passages that are used in each lesson are chosen with the appropriate context in mind, and are not simply proof texts. I have tried to avoid passages taken completely out of context. My hope is that this guide will be helpful for men's ministries and men's study groups. May God direct your steps!

Questions
Introduction

Questions and Thoughts
◇◇◇◇◇◇◇◇◇◇◇◇◇◇◇◇◇◇◇◇◇◇◇◇◇◇◇◇◇◇◇

Read Numbers 13:1–14:9.

1. How many men were sent on this assignment to explore Canaan?

2. How many men finished their assignment strongly?

3. Who were those that finished their assigned task strongly?

4. What beliefs separated them from the rest of the pack?

5. Please cite the verses from this passage that help you to answer this question.

Biblical scholars report that few biblical leaders in Scripture finished well. The same is true for Christian leaders and men today. In fact, it is worse today than in biblical times. Estimates range from 80 to 90 percent of men today finish poorly.

6. Does this surprise you? Why?

7. Who are some of the men in your life who finished well?

8. Who are some of the men in your life who didn't
    finish well?

9. Have you thought about the *offensive* and *defensive*
    aspects of preparing for finishing strongly?

The Bible connects beliefs with behaviors in the following ways:

- What we believe;
- This is tested by the trials of life;
- Those tests result in convictions;
- Those convictions become attitudes;
- Those attitudes then translate into behaviors.

Taking the information from above about how beliefs are
connected to behaviors, think through and fill out the following
chart.

Belief-to-behavior connections	How did Caleb and Joshua respond?	How did the other ten spies respond?
What they BELIEVED		
Was TESTED by the trials of life		
Those tests resulted in CONVICTIONS		
Those convictions became ATTITUDES		
Those attitudes then translated into BEHAVIORS		

10. Do you recognize the need to change from within
    (mind, heart, and will)?

11. Will you pray and ask God's help to be on track to
    finish strong?

Questions 1

Take Your Finish Seriously
◇◇◇

1. After reading Chapter 1, what are the differences between a competitive track race and life's race?

2. Are there additional differences that you can think of?

3. What are the similarities between life's race and other competitive races?

4. From what Bill told you about Art Armour, please think through and fill out the belief-to-behavior connection for Art.

Belief-to-behavior connections	How did Arthur respond?
What did he BELIEVE?	
What TESTS came in his life?	
Those tests resulted in what CONVICTIONS?	
Those convictions became what ATTITUDES?	
Those attitudes then translated into what BEHAVIORS?	

Bill provides a suggested prayer in this chapter:

God, please enable me to finish my life in a way that brings glory to You. Help me to avoid any moral failures that I know I am prone to wander into, enable me to cultivate my appetites for godly virtues, give me the strength and wisdom to say no to those appetites that will harm me, my family, my church, my friends, my community, and, most importantly, You. Search my heart and see if there is any evil way within me and give me the will and dependence on You to stifle that evil. Cultivate within me an ever-growing affection for You and relationship with You. Give me the energy and stamina to run though life's finish line in a way that will please You and be useful to the Kingdom. I want to finish strong! In Christ's name I pray, Amen.

5. What is your reaction to the prayer that Bill suggests?

6. Do you see yourself as prone to failures of any kind?

7. How would you describe your affections and appetites?

8. Do you like the idea of being dependent on someone else? What about dependence on God?

9. Is the cultivation of your affections and appetites something that you have considered? Explain further.

10. Have you considered that to finish strong means not only church life, but home life, hobby life, work life, and, in fact, all of life?

11. Have you ever known anyone like Arthur Armour? Explain further.

Questions 2

You Must Be Born Again
◇◇◇◇◇◇◇◇◇◇◇◇◇◇◇◇◇◇◇◇◇◇◇◇◇◇◇◇◇◇◇◇◇◇◇◇

Please read the entire account of Jesus and Nicodemus (John 3:1–21). Do your best to put yourself in Nicodemus' shoes to think and feel as he must have felt on this night.

1. Why did Nicodemus come to Jesus at night?

2. Have you ever felt that if you became a born-again Christian, then some people whom you considered important might think unkindly of you?

3. The gospel accounts tell us what Jesus said and did prior to His night meeting with Nicodemus. Nicodemus also knew these same facts and he believed them to be true. He lived in Jesus' day and had every means of verifying the truth of Jesus' teachings and deeds. Nicodemus' statement in verse 2 is not a question, yet Jesus answers as if it was. Why?

4. What did Jesus mean when He told Nicodemus that "unless one is born again he cannot see the kingdom of God"?

5. What are the two kinds of birth that Jesus explains?

6. If you had been in Nicodemus' shoes, what would you be feeling as you conversed with Jesus?

7. Have you ever felt similar feelings when hearing people speak about the biblical truths of the gospel?

8. Verse 14 refers to an event that occurred in the wilderness while Israel was being led to the Promised land. The Israelites complained bitterly and sinfully, and God sent a plague of snakes to deal with the culprits. The snakes killed grumblers. Moses prayed and gave the people a way to save themselves from God's wrath. Moses raised a pole made with a snake image on its end, and all the people had to do was believe Moses' words from God, "Everyone who is bitten, when he sees it [the snake on the pole], shall live." In simple words, "Believe and look at the snake on the pole and you will thereby live."

9. For what purpose is Jesus causing this Jewish teacher to recall the history of Israel?

10. The world says that "seeing is believing." However, verses 16–18 say what?

11. Why do people not believe Jesus' gospel according to verses 19–21?

12. What is it that verses 19–21 speak of as one of the benefits of the gospel?

13. If you put yourself in Nicodemus' shoes, then how would you have responded to Jesus' dialog?

Questions 3

You Must Know the Goal of a Strong Finish

Some people are naturally goal-oriented and respond well to disciplined, focused objectives. Others, on the opposite end of the spectrum, like to think of themselves as free-spirited individuals not bound by aims that seem to put them into a box. Obviously, there are many variations in between and surrounding these two approaches.

1. Do you know where you might fit on this matrix of approaches to finishing goals?

It is important that you know yourself on this spectrum. If you are married and having trouble deciding, then ask your wife for her opinion.

2. Read Philippians 3:1–15. Look at verses 1–6. What is Paul saying that is not his goal?

3. Paul's former Jewish teachers put value on those things that Paul now considers as losses. What are now his primary goals as he states them in verse 8–11? Summarize them on the table on the following page.

Verse 8	
Verse 9	
Verse 9	
Verse 10	
Verse 10	
Verse 10	

4. Does what Paul say about himself in verse 12a surprise you? Have you ever felt this way?

5. What are the things that Paul says he will be doing to seek his spiritual maturity in verses 12–14?

6. Are you doing these things? Explain.

7. Paul repeats a three-word phrase twice in verses 12 and 14. What is the phrase? What does it teach us?

8. What is it in verse 15 that Paul is asking the Philippian people to do?

9. What is the corrective measure that Paul reminds the Philippians will be taken if their thinking is amiss?

10. Who is it that will take the initiative on this measure?

11. Paul had become a new creation. Bill emphasizes the importance of "becoming" and the "doing" being an outgrowth of the becoming. Do you understand that and see how that truth developed in Paul's life as he matured?

12. Do you agree with that for your life? If so, why? If not, why not?

13. Have you prayed that God would show you the way to "becoming"?

Questions 4

Run Your Race, Not Someone Else's

◇◇◇

Read Hebrews 12:1–11.

1. Who are the people in "the cloud of witnesses"? If you are having trouble answering this question, read Hebrews chapter 11.

2. What are two defensive strategies in verse 1 that the Hebrew writer gives to his readers?

3. How does the writer of Hebrews describe the race that his readers are to run?

4. How does this reinforce the principle put forth in Chapter 4?

5. What does verse 2 tell us about where our faith originates and who will bring it to perfection?

6. Do you believe what the writer of Hebrews is telling you, or do you believe that you are the originator of your faith and that you alone can bring yourself to maturity?

7. When you look to role models—which is often a good thing to do—have you occasionally assumed that you must do everything the same way as they have?

8. Do you understand that an undue focus on a specific role model can result in trying to run that person's

race instead of yours? This can happen with a friend, a father, an uncle, or a business cohort.

9. Verses 3–11 speak about the Lord's discipline. Because of some folks' experiences with abusive "disciplines," these verses can often be hurtful or dismissive. Please know that most often when the New Testament speaks of discipline, it is referring to it as teaching, training, and the like—not physical punishment.

10. What is your reaction to the connotation of the word "discipline"? (The term *connotation* means an idea or feeling that a word invokes in addition to its literal or primary meaning.)

11. Have you thought about how this may filter the way that you perceive God?

12. Bill will testify that it took him many years to let go of making everything a competition, and believes that until the day he dies he will struggle with changing his thinking on this issue. Therefore, Bill makes a point of focusing onsetting a best time for one's self, not winning competitively against anyone else, because he sees this as a healthier way to grow in Christ, and at the same time develop healthy people relationships.

13. Do you struggle with the concept of focusing on "best times"?

14. Is this concept foreign to you? If so, then explain how.

15. Do you believe that the way that you run the race of life is a serious pursuit? Explain why.

16. Whatever your shortcomings are in running your race, have you considered the fact that the root causes of those shortcomings are faulty biblical beliefs?

17. Are you willing to pray and ask God to show you where your biblical beliefs are faulty?

Questions 5

Be Satisfied with Progress;
Don't Expect Perfection
◇◇◇◇◇◇◇◇◇◇◇◇◇◇◇◇◇◇◇◇◇◇◇◇◇◇◇◇◇◇◇◇◇◇

1. Perfectionism is a common malady. Some people struggle with it in every area of life. Some only pursue it in one area—work, art, music, sports, cleanliness, etc.

2. Do you struggle with perfectionism?

3. Do you sometimes beat yourself up when you fail at a particular task or project?

4. Revisit Paul's words in Philippians 3:12–14, and then add to them John 3:19–21.

5. Does Paul consider himself to be perfect?

6. What is his response to his imperfection?

7. Why does he do the things he does? Is it anything he has done? Or has someone done something to him?

8. Have you actually spent any time considering just how far off perfection most of us are?

9. Have you considered that even when we have completed a very virtuous assignment, if we were to carefully examine our motives, they might be quite tainted?

10. One of the wonderful beauties of what God has done for us is expressed in John 3:19–21. Can you identify it?

11. If you are having trouble finding it, then let me lead you a bit. Look at verse 20. What is it that unbelievers fear?

12. Then, by implication, in all three verses, what is it that we, as genuine believers know is true about our deeds and our God, that sets us free from this fear?

13. Can you celebrate this gracious gift from God and the freedom it brings?

14. Expectations are very important for most people. How do you react to the reality that you will never have a perfect day? Maybe never a perfect hour? Maybe never a perfect minute?

15. Will you pray that God would lead you to a place where you can be satisfied with progress, not perfection?

Questions 6

Focus on What You Can Become, Not on What You Have Done

◇◇◇◇◇◇◇◇◇◇◇◇◇◇◇◇◇◇◇◇◇◇◇◇◇◇◇◇◇◇◇◇◇◇

1. If someone asked you this question, how would you answer it? "Who is the greatest in the kingdom of heaven?"

Now, read Matthew 18:1–4 and then respond to the questions that are asked.

2. What is the question the disciples ask Jesus?

3. What might you have expected Jesus' answer to be?

4. Does Jesus' answer surprise you?

5. What are the verbs in verse 3 that describe what the entry requirements are for the Kingdom?

6. How does verse 4 help explain what Jesus meant?

7. How does this verse help explain what Jesus meant? (Clue: what does Jesus say and then what does the child do?)

8. So when Jesus says we are to be "like" or "as" little children, what does He mean?

Read Mark 1:16–17. (Note: please use any version other than the NIV for these verses; the NIV leaves out an important word for our point.)

9.   What is Jesus' command?

10. What does Jesus say He will do for Peter and Andrew?

11. Do you believe that He can and will do the same for you?

Read John 1:10–13.

12. What right does Jesus give to believers in verse 12?

13. Have you noticed the emphasis on "becoming" in the passages noted?

14. In the world, as you have experienced it, what have you been rewarded for: becoming or doing?

15. How do you think these experiences impact your understanding of how God evaluates and accepts you?

16. How foreign do you think it is for most men to ask them to place their emphasis on "being" and "becoming," not on "doing"?

17. Do you really understand what it means that you are a "new spiritual creation"?

18. How do you react to the offensive and defensive elements of Paul's comments cited at the end of chapter 6?

19. Are you willing to pray and ask God to help you see and understand what it means to be a new creation, and begin to learn what it means in everyday terms to "become"?

20. Are you willing to pray and ask God to help you

see and experience the reality that, if you become different, then you will behave differently?

21. Can you imagine the freedom from false guilt that understanding "becoming" provides?

Questions 7

Become More Dependent on God and Less Independent
◇◇◇◇◇◇◇◇◇◇◇◇◇◇◇◇◇◇◇◇◇◇◇◇◇◇◇◇◇◇◇◇◇

1. Do you like John Wayne's movies?

2. Does the idea of being dependent on anyone (especially a someone whom you cannot see or touch or call on the phone) strike a discordant note in you?

3. What are some of the reasons that men, in particular, do not want to be dependent?

4. Is there some sinful (or perhaps annoying) behavior that you have that you would describe as follows? "This is just the way that God has made me and I will always be this way, no matter what."

5. Have you ever considered that you may not be able to change that behavior, but that the Spirit of God who lives with you can? How is He able to do that?

6. Have you ever taken the risk to ask God to change your behavior and let Him have His way? What keeps you from taking that risk?

Read Acts 5:12–42.

7. Remembering that these apostles just months before had scattered in fear when Jesus was arrested, observe and discuss what these same apostles are able to do in these verses.

8. What kind of opposition did they face?

9. What kind of physical pain did they endure?

10. How had their speech been impacted?

11. What does verse 32 tell us that helps us understand the change that transformed these men?

Read 2 Corinthians 12:9–10.

12. How do these words of Paul help us to understand how God was going to receive glory from the apostles' transformation?

13. Will you pray, asking God to help you accept your dependence on Him for becoming what you need to become?

Questions 8

Take Responsibility for Your Household and Recognize God As Your Only Real Judge

Read Ephesians 5:1–6:9. Paul often follows a pattern in his letters. He begins with theology—what we should believe. He then ends with what we should do with theology—that is, the behavior that flows from the theology. Paul uses this pattern in Ephesians, where the first three chapters consist of theology. Then, starting with chapter 4, he begins to discuss the behavior that rightly should follow.

1. What is the command in verse 1 of chapter 5?

2. What is the instruction in verse 21?

3. In a home with a husband and a wife to whom does this apply?

4. What is the instruction to wives in verse 22a?

5. Does verse 22a instruct women to submit to all men?

6. In what way do verses 22b–24 instruct a wife to submit to her husband? What is the analogy (comparison) that Paul uses?

7. What is the instruction to husbands in verse 25a?

8. In what way do verses 25b–28 instruct a husband to love his wife?

9. What is the analogy (comparison) that Paul uses?

10. How many verses does Paul devote to the instruction of the wife and how many does he devote to the instruction of the husband?

11. What does your answer tell you?

12. Which instruction seems the most difficult?

13. Look at verse 32 carefully. How does it help instruct both husband and wife as to the most important aspects of the assigned godly role as a spouse?

There are several words that come to mind concerning Paul's instruction: submission; acquiescence; bullying; overbearance. Make sure that you know what each of those words mean and how they apply (or do not apply) to Paul's teaching.

Please read the following verses.

- Acts 10:42. "And he commanded us to preach to the people and to testify that he (Jesus) is the one appointed by God to be judge of the living and the dead."
- Acts 17:30–31. "The times of ignorance God overlooked, but now he commands all people everywhere to repent, because he has fixed a day on which he will judge the world in righteousness by a man whom he has appointed; and of this he has given assurance to all by raising him from the dead."
- 2 Timothy 4:1. "I charge you in the presence of God and of Christ Jesus, who is to judge the living and the dead, and by his appearing and his kingdom."

14. Who is the judge in each of these verses?

Please read the following verses.

- Acts 5:27–29. "And when they had brought them [Peter and the apostles], they set them before the council. And the high priest questioned them, saying, 'We strictly charged you not to teach in this name, yet here you have filled Jerusalem with your teaching, and you intend to bring this man's blood upon us.' But Peter and the apostles answered, 'We must obey God rather than men.'"

15. What do you take away from these verses?

16. Are you preparing yourself for the day when you may have to act with the same resolve as Peter and the apostles?

17. What or who will give you the courage and words to do so?

18. Why do you suppose it is important, ahead of time, to think through a circumstance like this and prepare for the way you will respond?

Questions 9

To Finish Strong, You Must Think Biblically

Read 2 Timothy 1:3–8, 11–14; 2:14–15; and 3:10–4:5. Remember that Paul, a pastor, is instructing his protégé, Timothy, who is also a pastor. The instructions are first applicable for pastors, but they are also useful for every believer in every age who wants to be mature in his faith.

1. Where did Timothy's faith begin (verse 1:5)?

2. What are the verbs in verse 1:5?

3. Which ones describe the faith of Timothy, his mother, and grandmother?

4. What do these verbs tell you about the depth of faith that these three people had?

5. What is Timothy instructed to not be ashamed of in verse 8 of chapter 1?

6. What is Timothy to follow according to 1:13?

7. Where is Timothy to get the power to carry out his guarding according to verse 1:14?

8. What is the thing that Timothy is to guard (1:14)?

9. What does Paul instruct Timothy to do and become in verse 2:15a?

10. How does verse 2:15b help define what Paul wants Timothy to become?

11. What is the "truth" that Paul refers to in verse 2:15c?

12. Summarize verse 2:15 in ten or fewer words.

Look carefully at verses 3:14–16. They are rich for our purposes here.

13. What is Timothy to continue in (3:14)?

14. What or who are the sources of his learning (3:14)?

15. What has Timothy been taught by his grandmother and mother since he was a child (3:15)?

16. What are the sacred writings (3:15)?

17. What will the sacred writings attain (3:15)? Through what?

18. How much of Scripture is from God (3:16)?

19. What is Scripture profitable for (3:16)?

20. What do each of those things identified as profitable mean in twenty-first-century churches (3:16)?

21. What do the Scriptures accomplish (3:17)?

22. By implication, then, from what Paul says, can you be mature in your faith and not know all Scripture?

23. From what Paul implies in chapter 3, how full is one's tool box to do good works if one's knowledge of Scripture is a pittance?

24. According to verse 4:2, what is Timothy to do with his knowledge of Scripture?

25. What kinds of teachers does Paul prophesy about in verse 4:3?

26. In conclusion, consider this question: "How does all this apply to you?"

Questions 10

Be Willing to Die to Self, and Act on That Willingness
◇◇◇◇◇◇◇◇◇◇◇◇◇◇◇◇◇◇◇◇◇◇◇◇◇◇◇◇◇◇◇◇◇◇◇

Read Matthew 10:34–39, 16:24–28; Mark 8:27–38; Luke 9:18–27

1. The Spirit of God has the Gospel writers repeat a similar history four times. What does that tell you?

2. In Matthew 10, is Jesus saying that, as believers, we should hate our families?

3. At the time that Jesus lived, what would it have meant to "take up your cross and follow" Jesus?

4. At that time, what kind of commitment would that have taken?

5. Do you think that the level of commitment today that God expects has changed?

6. What does Jesus mean in Matthew 16:24–25?

7. What is the extra verb that is added to verse 24 that makes it even more challenging?

8. What does Jesus mean when He says "lose your life"?

9. What does Jesus liken it to, if a person chooses to stay with the world and possibly gain everything the world has to offer?

10. What is the motivation that Jesus speaks of in Matthew 16:27?

11. What does Luke add to the warning of what will happen if one chooses to reject Christ in 9:26?

12. Notice that, in the Luke and Mark passages, they begin with Jesus asking the questions, "Who do the people say that I am?" and "Who do you say that I am?" Why is the second question so important for the disciples to have to answer?

13. Why is this same question important for us to answer?

14. If we answer it correctly, as Peter did, how does that relate to dying to self?

15. If we not only answer correctly but also respond to what we say we believe, how will our behaviors change over time?

16. If there is no change in behaviors, what does that say?

17. What is your reaction to being asked to die to self?

18. How does that fit into today's American culture?

Questions 11

Commit to Finishing Strong
◇◇◇

Read Genesis 12:1–5.

1. How old was Abram when he was called by God to leave his homeland and travel to a county he had never seen before?

2. What kinds of relationships would Abram have developed in those years? Business? Religious? Family? Friends? Hobbies?

3. If you had been a fly on the wall in Abram's dining room, what do you imagine the conversations were like between him and Sarai when he told her that he was considering moving the family to a place he had never seen since he had been called by a God whom they had never heard from before?

4. Have you ever moved from one location to another?

5. How hard was that for you?

6. How much harder was it for your wife?

7. Do you think that things were different for Abram and Sarai?

8. Have you heard Christian couples say they would never move from the place they were born or are currently living?

9. Which of these Old Testament characters had to move? Adam and Eve? Abram? Jacob? Isaac? David? Joshua? Moses?

10. Is our commitment as believers to a place or to God?

11. What is your attitude toward moving?

12. What is it that we as believers have in Christ that allows us to be able to move geographically and still have our foundation firmly planted?

13. What purpose does a conscious commitment play in the life of any human being?

14. In our culture today in America, what cultural barriers are there to committing to anything 100 percent?

15. What do some people in our society call people who are 100 percent committed to Christ?

16. Does what people may call you impact you?

17. Are you willing to commit 100 percent to Christ?

18. What is there about that commitment that might scare you away from taking that step?

Questions 12

Develop a Mind For the Things of God

Read Romans 8:1–9, 12:1–3; Ephesians 4:17–27; 1 Peter 1:13–16.

1. In Romans 8:5, what does Paul say the Roman believers are supposed to do with their minds?

2. By contrast, what does Paul say unbelievers set their minds on?

3. Paul equates setting one's mind on the things of God to what two things in verse 8:6?

4. Are these two things important to you?

5. What does Paul say that the Roman believers are to do in 12:2?

6. How does he say they are to accomplish that in verse 2?

Verbs have either an active voice or passive voice. In the active voice, the subject of the sentence is doing the acting. In the passive voice, the subject is being acted upon. In verse 2 of chapter 12, the subject is assumed to be you, the Roman believers plural.

7. In verse 2b is the verb active or passive?

8. What does this tell us about how this transformation will take place?

9. What role does a person's will play in this process? Remember that our wills are like rheostats (dimmer-switches) that can be regulated from barely on to full power.

10. What is it that Romans 12:2 tells you will be able to gain by the testing of the renewal of your mind?

11. In your own words, what is it that verse 12:3 warns against?

12. What does Ephesians 4:17–27 tell you about an unconverted mind and a genuine believer's mind?

13. Paul tells the Ephesian believers to put something off and put something on. What does he mean by that statement?

14. How does this relate to a believer's mind?

15. Summarize in your own words Peter's instructions to believers in 1 Peter 1:13–15.

16. What have you learned by looking at all these verses that you can internalize and believe, and then act upon?

Questions 13

Develop God-Pleasing Appetites and Passions
◇◇

Reread 1 Peter 1:13–15 and Ephesians 4:17–27. Read Luke 12:1–31.

1. What does Peter mean when he says, "prepare your minds" (1 Peter 1:13)?

2. What does Peter mean when he says, "being sober minded" (1 Peter 1:13)?

3. What does Peter mean when he says, "the revelation of Jesus" (1 Peter 1:13)?

4. What does the revelation of Jesus bring or give to you (1 Peter 1:13)?

5. What does Peter instruct his readers to flee from and what does he instruct them to pursue (1 Peter 1:14)?

6. In Ephesians 4:20–21, Paul makes an assumption about the Ephesian believers. What is it?

7. Why is this such an important starting point?

8. Where (or from whom) would the Ephesian believers have learned this?

9. Where may we learn this?

10. Why is our position and opportunity to learn these truths even more advantageous than the Ephesian believers?

11. Describe the way that Paul characterizes the "old self."

12. In Ephesians 4:23, where does Paul say renewal begins?

13. Does this surprise you?

14. In Luke 12 starting in verse 1, who is Jesus speaking to?

15. What is Jesus telling his disciples to flee from and what is he telling them to pursue?

16. Starting in verse 13, the audience changes. Who, now, is the audience?

17. In Luke 12:14–26, what is Jesus telling His audience to flee from, and what is He telling them to pursue?

18. In Luke 12:27–31, what groups of things is Jesus telling His audience to flee from and what groups of things is He telling them to pursue?

19. What do you conclude about fleeing and pursuing?

20. Where will you discover what should be on the flee-list and what should be on the pursue-list?

21. Have these passages changed your thinking in any way? How? Or why not?

22. What will you pray about after reading these passages?

23. What is in your control and what can you depend upon from God?

Questions 14

Develop a "Habit Pattern" Mindset

Read Daniel 6.

1.   How did Daniel's enemies describe him?

2.   What was it that his enemies could predict because his godly habits were so engrained?

3.   How did God reward his godly habits and obedience?

4.   How did Daniel's behavior impact the King?

5.   One thing is often missed in chapter 6. Daniel had been identified by the King to do what in verse 3?

6.   His enemies had him thrown into the lions' den assuming he would be killed. What happened to them in verse 24?

7.   If the riffraff of the King's administration needed purging, then what had God accomplished by this ordeal for Daniel that he may have never been able to accomplish for himself?

Read these veses from Psalm 119.

> 30 I have chosen the way of faithfulness; I set your rules before me.
> 31 I cling to your testimonies, O LORD; let me not be put to shame!

32 I will run in the way of your commandments when you enlarge my heart!
40 Behold, I long for your precepts; in your righteousness give me life!
44 I will keep your law continually, forever and ever,
45 and I shall walk in a wide place, for I have sought your precepts.
47 for I find my delight in your commandments, which I love.
48 I will lift up my hands toward your commandments, which I love, and I will meditate on your statutes.
51 The insolent utterly deride me, but I do not turn away from your law.

8. What are they saying about the psalmist's habits that he is forming?

9. What principles can you glean from the psalmist?

10. You can also look at these verses to add to your understanding: 54, 55, 56, 60, 67, 69, 100, 101, 102, 105, 106, 110, 112, 166, 167, 168.

11. Some people react to the idea of developing habit patterns negatively, seeing them as straightjackets or tethers on their freedom and creativity. How do you react to the idea of developing spiritual habit patterns?

12. How well did habit patterns serve Daniel?

13. Did Jesus have habit patterns?

14. Have you ever analyzed the Gospel accounts to see how many times Jesus prayed? Did He pray before every major decision and milestone in His ministry? How many times does it say that the disciples looked for Him and found Him praying?

15. Describe your habit pattern of praying.

Questions that are personal:

16. When you are faced with a dilemma, like making a critical decision, where do you go for advice and counsel?

17. Is your motivation always to make your decisions in the best way for the Kingdom and your Savior, or are other perks and rewards more important to you?

18. Are you moved more by what other people will think or feel than what God approves?

19. Do you even think of God when faced with a dilemma?

20. When faced with the prospect of lying or telling the truth do you always tell the truth?

21. Are you missing the peace that passes all understanding that comes with knowing your response is always to tell the truth?

22. When tempted to cheat, do you ever consider it as a legitimate option?

23. If no one is looking do you believe you are safe to do whatever you can get away with?

Questions 15

Know Your Greatest Enemy:
Sexual Immorality
◇◇◇◇◇◇◇◇◇◇◇◇◇◇◇◇◇◇◇◇◇◇◇◇◇◇

Read Job 31:1; Proverbs 4:24–27, 17:24; Matthew 5:27–30.

1. What is the commitment that Job made with himself mentioned in Job 31:1?

2. In practical terms today, what does that mean? What does it not mean?

3. How would such a commitment be helpful in fighting the enemy of improper sexual thoughts?

4. How would such a commitment impact the thought of viewing pornography in any form?

5. How do the two passages from Proverbs encourage us to flee certain things and pursue certain other things?

Jesus addresses adultery in the Sermon on the Mount.

6. What does Jesus call intentional lustful thoughts about a woman?

7. Where are these thoughts to have taken place?

8. How many of us can profess that we have never committed this sin?

9. Do you consider this sin serious?

10. Did Jesus?

11. Why else would He have mentioned it this way?

12. Why do you suppose that He dealt with it in this way?

13. Is Jesus really recommending that we mutilate our bodies?

Read 1 Corinthians 6:12–20.

14. What is the physical body made for and does God consider it important?

15. How does Paul describe the body?

16. What was the Temple meant to be for the Jewish nation?

17. What does Paul say your body is?

18. How does this put a completely different light on sexual sin of any kind?

Read Genesis 39:1–20.

19. How does Joseph decline Potiphar's wife's invitation to sleep with her in verses 8–9?

20. How does Joseph describe adultery in verse 9?

21. How does this differ from the way we describe adultery in our culture today?

22. How does the modern description of adultery impact how we think about it?

23. What does Joseph do when he is trapped in a circumstance of sexual immorality described in verse 12?

24. What does this suggest to us as an appropriate way to deal with some sexual situations?

25. What are your personal sexual temptations?

26. Have you taken these temptations to the Lord for His help?

Questions 16

Know Your Enemies #2 and #3:
Love of Money and Love of Power

◇◇◇◇◇◇◇◇◇◇◇◇◇◇◇◇◇◇◇◇◇◇◇◇◇◇◇◇◇◇◇◇◇◇◇◇◇◇

Read Hebrews 13:1–6; Deuteronomy 31:1–8.

1. What are the two instructions that Hebrews 5a gives?

2. Look at Deuteronomy 31 verses 6 and 8. What three ideas are repeated in both verses?

3. Where or from whom did these ideas originate?

4. Now look at Hebrews 13:5b "he has said." Who is the "he" that the Hebrews writer refers to?

5. For what reason does the Hebrews writer say that we can be content and keep our lives free from the love of money in verse 5b?

6. Put all this together. What does God say is the root cause of "love of money" and "lack of contentment"?

7. In what ways does this truth strike you personally? If not why not?

Read Mark 8:27–38.

8. In verse 29, Jesus asks the disciples, "Who do you say I am?" What is Peter's answer?

9. What did being the "Christ" or "Messiah" mean at that very time to Peter?

10. With your answer in mind, why then does Peter rebuke Jesus when He says that He will be rejected and must die?

11. What does Jesus' reply to Peter in verse 33 have to do with earthly power?

12. What do verses 36–37 have to do with money and power?

Read James 4:13–17.

13. How does James describe the statement made in verse 13? (Hint: look at verse 16.)

14. When we say something like, "We plan to go to a certain place and make a profit and assume that God will bless us in it," what are we doing? Is it sin?

15. What do verses 14–15 tell us about who it is that enables us to do what we can do?

Read 1 Timothy 6:6–11, 17–19.

16. Where does Paul tell Timothy there is great gain in verse 6?

17. What risk does Paul say exists for those who desire to be rich in verse 9?

18. What does Paul say is the root of all kinds of evil in verse 10?

19. Paul gives the "love of money" another description in verse 10b. What is that description?

20. What traps for the rich does Paul delineate in verse 17?

21. How does Paul describe what is "truly life" in verses 18–19?

Questions 17

Biblical Warnings to Heed

It is important to apply these warnings to yourself and not think of them as applying to someone else. So as you reflect upon them, please consider how they relate (apply) to you.

1. How good a listener are you?

2. James tells us to be slow to speak and quick to listen. Does this describe you?

3. Does it matter to you who gives you the warning? Are there people from whom you may reject a warning, just because it came from them?

4. There are eight warnings given. Which two or three of those are most challenging for you?

5. Which two or three would your wife or best friends recommend for you?

6. Does it surprise you that Jesus was not born with encyclopedic knowledge of everything, but instead had to progressively learn just as you and I do?

7. If Jesus had to learn as He grew, how much more do we need to keep learning as we grow?

8. There are branches of professing Christians who believe that once they are saved, they become sinless. Have you completely or partially been enticed by this delusion?

9. Are you comfortable knowing that, on this side of heaven, you will never be perfected in your behavior and thinking?

There is a saying that "Jesus paid a debt He didn't owe, so that sinners may be freed from a debt they could never repay." It is based on 2 Corinthians 5:21: "For our sake he made him to be sin who knew no sin, so that in him we might become the righteousness of God."

10. Is it difficult for you to accept the fact that in God's eyes you are perfect, and when He looks at you He sees Christ's perfect righteousness?

11. Is it hard for you to realize that you can do nothing that will earn your salvation and right standing before God?

12. Is your independence something that you value highly?

13. Is it difficult for you to accept your complete dependence on God?

There are several ways to view God as Judge. Three ways are described below.

• First, He is a taskmaster who is watching every move you make and just waiting to zap you when you make mistakes. He ignores nothing and punishes all faults.
• Second, He is a loving Father who desires that you become mature, and He takes every opportunity to use His Word, His providence, and your mistakes to develop you to maturity, even if it may involve some discomfort or pain.
• Third, He is a God who sees everything, and loves His own so much, that once they are a part of His family they

may behave and think freely, because He has set them free.

14. Which of these views most closely agrees with how you view God as Judge?

15. How does the way you view God as Judge impact everything you do?

16. There is a saying among some Christians that goes something like this, "God has a wonderful plan for your life!" How is that statement true and false at the same time?

17. How can that statement lead some professing Christians to be disillusioned?

18. Did Jesus ever say anything like this to His disciples?

19. Would you describe the earthly end of life experiences for the disciples as "wonderful?"

20. How do you react to God when all things around you are crumbling?

According to Proverbs 6:16–19, there are six things that the LORD hates, seven that are an abomination to him:

- haughty eyes,
- a lying tongue, and
- hands that shed innocent blood,
- a heart that devises wicked plans,
- feet that make haste to run to evil,
- a false witness who breathes out lies, and
- one who sows discord among brothers.

21. The first item on the list is "haughty eyes." What does haughty mean?

22. Who can have this kind of look?

23. What does it tell you that "haughty eyes" is first on God's list?

24. How does this list equate to problems in your church body?

25. Do your best to explain why you think these sins are offensive in God's eyes.

26. What is your attitude toward hard work?

27. If you had to show a record to your study group of the hours of work you put in over the last four weeks, how would that record reveal the answer to the question, "What is your attitude toward hard work?"

28. Past behavior is the best predictor of future behavior and the most accurate answer to what you really believe. What would your behavior reveal about what you believe about sloth?

Appendix 3

Leader's Addendum

An Addendum for Those Who Aspire (or Are Called) to Leadership Positions

Why This Addendum?

Leaders have unique privileges, responsibilities, challenges, and temptations. This addendum has been added to the original printing of *ENDURE: A Christian Man's Guide to Finishing Strong* to address a few of the issues that apply to men in leadership. This is not meant to be a comprehensive treatment of leadership, but is meant to highlight issues unique to Christian leaders that may not be addressed in books solely targeted at *leadership* in a more general way.

Many who will use this book are men in positions of leadership in business, education, medicine, the arts, ministry, and more. Their titles will range from Chief Executive Officer, Owner, to Front Line Supervisor in the manufacturing trades, and from Deacon, Elder, Senior Pastor to Sunday School Teacher in the church. Each discipline has its own titles, and every position of leadership has the opportunity to help others become fully committed followers of Jesus Christ. The hope and motive for this addendum is that it might be an additional encouragement, along with the main content of *Endure* and its *Study Guide*, for Christian leaders to finish well.

If you do not have a leader's title or position, but you are a husband or a father, this section will still apply to you. In God's eyes, your role as a husband and father is even more important than the obvious roles with high-sounding titles that seem to make the headlines. In a very real sense, every man who is married or has children is in a leadership position. I trust that you realize this!

Some may consider the husband's and father's role as somewhat "ho-hum," not worthy of mentioning. However, I am quite confident that God would disagree! From a biblical perspective, it is the most important leadership position in all of civilized society. A godly husband and father who leads his wife and children in a winsome, strong-but-meek, solidly scriptural manner with joy and humility performs a supernatural feat. This is no small accomplishment and no small task. Society today suffers from a dearth of this kind of leadership and would benefit greatly from men who fit this description.

So, if you find yourself thinking, "This is not for me; I am just a husband or just a father," please read on. These thoughts on leadership are definitely directed at you!

A

Be a Good Follower

Be ye followers of me, even as I also am of Christ.
1 Corinthians 11:1 (KJV)

It may seem strange to some to start words of encouragement for leaders with the statement, "Be a good follower." But that is precisely the place we should start.

The Argument for Being a Follower

Paul, one of the most outstanding leaders of the New Testament era, tells the people of the Corinthian church to be "followers" of him, just as he is a "follower" of Jesus. The Greek word used for follower can also be translated "imitator." So the message is clear, although it is seldom applied to leaders and leadership. In fact, some men in leadership positions might revolt at this thought. However, they would be mistaken. Scripture is consistently clear by example and precept that good following leads to good leadership. However, clarity does not always translate into behavior. For the majority of us, it is not the passages of Scripture that are unclear that give us the most trouble; it is the ones that are crystal clear.

My administrative assistant, Pat Leahy, once asked me this question: "What is the first and most important trait of Christian leadership?" I think that he was stunned at my quick response.

I said, "Be a good follower!"

I would like to say that my answer was based on 1 Corinthians 11. That would make me feel quite pious. But it would also make me a liar. Little did I know at the time that what I had been taught in Boy Scouts, sports, and the Naval Academy, and basic Bible knowledge had influenced my answer. The wisdom of God's message, by God's common grace, had penetrated even before I associated it directly with Paul's words to the Corinthians.

Here is a little background. I was eleven years old when I began Boy Scouts. I was immediately put under the tutelage of a patrol leader—a boy two years older than me. I became a follower and he led me to be a "Tenderfoot." That was a good title for the rank because, at that point in scouting, I knew nothing! I had a choice at that point to be a good follower, a happy-go-lucky follower, a miserable pain in the you-know-what follower, or several other choices. I chose to be an obedient follower. I loved scouting! The patrol leader helped me to advance, and I became a very good follower. Soon I became a patrol leader, leading other new Tenderfoot Scouts, then a Senior Patrol Leader, the leader of our troop, and later an Eagle Scout. The path to leadership began with my being a follower.

Team sports provided the same path to leadership. "Follow the lead of the coach" was the key to playing. Certain older players stood out as team leaders. "Follow their lead" was the next step. As I learned how to be a good follower of the coach and the competent older players, I was learning how to lead myself. The subsequent year, I became one of the leaders of the team. I had learned leadership by following.

The Naval Academy, in my day, did the same thing. As a Plebe (a freshman), I was lower than dirt—a true follower if there ever was one. There were four thousand young men at the Academy then, and three thousand of them were my seniors. Therefore, in Academy life, they qualified as my bosses. Imagine having three thousand bosses, aged nineteen to twenty-one years. Some were great! Some were pathetic! Squad leaders taught us, tested us, drilled us. They led. We followed. As a good follower, I became a leader. Every branch of the military service does something similar. The Marine Corps do the best job of developing leaders and they use the same pattern, perfected over time. The non-debatable point is that every leader begins as a follower.

The best examples of leaders who began as followers were Jesus' apostles. Rabbis in the first-century culture were highly sought after as teachers by young men. These young men applied to a rabbi to become a disciple and to study underneath him. The rabbi then culled the applicants much like universities do today. Jesus stood this process on its head. Unlike the other rabbis, Jesus took no applicants but rather selected His followers, just like He selects His followers today. They never applied to Him. Most were surprised that He called. These young men then became His primary followers. They abided with Him, listened to His teaching, observed His manner of speaking and acting, watched His living, learned from the way He dealt with different kinds of people, grew from His rebukes, were tested with on-the-job assignments, and marveled at His supernatural miracles. They did life together!

Because He chose them, spent time with them, and loved them, they were radically changed. Yet when Jesus was crucified, they scattered in fear. It was only after they were given the Holy Spirit that the Spirit reminded them of all they had been taught. The changes that had begun before Christ's death were now sealed! Completed! They then became the leaders of a new organism—the Church. They *became* powerful leaders. Three years as followers and then their leadership "turned the world upside down" (Acts 17:6).

The Heart of a Follower

The lessons that can be learned as a follower are crucial. More often than not, they are missed or overlooked or overshadowed by miserable bosses, mistreatment, or misunderstanding. Therefore, a true follower's heart is necessary.

I will start with poor behavior from good-hearted people. You may ask, "Why?" The answer is simple. Living life in the real world of sports, education, the military, business, and now church, all too often good-hearted people think they are behaving honorably, and yet they are not. So I trust that a couple of illustrations of poor behavior will be helpful.

Mark reports Peter's poor behavior in his Gospel account:

> He [Jesus] began to teach them [the disciples] that the
> Son of Man must suffer many things and be rejected by
> the elders and the chief priests and the scribes and be
> killed, and after three days rise again. And he [Jesus]
> said this plainly. And Peter took him aside and began
> to rebuke him. But turning and seeing his disciples, he
> rebuked Peter and said, "Get behind me, Satan! For you
> are not setting your mind on the things of God, but on the
> things of man."
> (Mark 8:31–33)

The apostle Peter obviously had a good heart. Good hearts
can do good things, but sadly they can also do bad things. That
is why this illustration is so helpful to us. The good-hearted
Peter displayed a poor follower's behavior. If this can happen
to Peter after almost two years of instruction from Jesus Himself, we should be humble enough to realize that we can also
stumble as he did.

Here is the second illustration: Jamie, a friend of mine,
exhibited a similar sort of poor behavior. He was asked to
serve on a building committee at our church. He was not supposed to be the leader, but was an important contributing
team member. After a few months, he came to me with the
following report; it led to a further discussion between us:

"Bill, Alonzo, the building committee leader, is incompe-
tent. He doesn't know how to run a meeting, the meetings are
too long, and as a result we hardly get anything done in the
time we spend there. Even though we seem to be making progress, our progress is at a snail's pace. I don't like the direction
we are going and I don't like Alonzo's style of leadership."

I asked, "Have you discussed this with Alonzo?"

Very quickly Jamie replied, "No! Why would I do that?"

I then asked him, "What have you done to help Alonzo?"

"Not much," Jamie stated. "He doesn't give us much of a chance."

Whether Jamie realized it or not, and whether Peter realized it or not, they were both bristling at the idea of being a follower, and therefore behaving in an unacceptable manner as a follower. Their hearts were not right yet. Their implicit assumption was that their primary responsibility was to evaluate the leader, his instructions, his actions, and his decisions, and then take appropriate action where necessary. They were assuming that they knew as much, if not more, than the leader whom they were following. They were wrong on both counts.

Please do not get me wrong. I am not saying, "Do whatever your leader says without thinking." I am not implying that a good-hearted follower always blindly follows what the leader says. That is wrong-headed and can lead to drastic consequences. The Word of God and the Spirit of God do not leave us as believers empty-handed with no guidance in this matter. They provide us with a wonderful plumb line of truth to guide us. We ought always to use it. Does the instruction violate a biblical truth? The things that Peter and Jamie were bristling against were not violations of biblical truth; they were matters of opinion.

In Peter's case, he was usurping God Himself. He knew little of the plan of God, understood even less at the time, and trusted in his own judgment far too generously. We can do the same, and often do. We are quite good at convincing ourselves of the merits of our own knowledge and reasoning.

In the illustration of my friend, Jamie, he assumed he knew the overall plan, but he did not. He assumed that he was the judge of the timeline, when he was not, and he assumed that he was tasked with the responsibility to evaluate his leader's management style, which was presumptive. None of the above responsibilities was given to him, and the issues that troubled him were not biblical issues. On top of that, he was blind to the fact that he had ignored a biblical instruction.

> If your brother sins against you, go and tell him his fault,
> between you and him alone. If he listens to you, you have
> gained your brother.
> (Matthew 18:15)

He perceived that Alonzo was performing poorly and leading in a unhealthy manner. The biblical thing to do was to speak first with Alonzo. He should have approached his brother, speaking the truth with love and gentleness as Paul instructed, and voiced his opinion. He never said a word to Alonzo. Instead he went around to his superior—me. He was quick to condemn the "fault" in his leader, while he had a "larger fault" in his own behavior.

So what does the heart of a good follower look like? Three passages of Scripture highlight what a good heart should look like.

> You shall love the LORD your God with all your heart and
> with all your soul and with all your might.
> (Deuteronomy 6:5)

> And you, Solomon my son, know the God of your father
> and serve him with a whole heart and with a willing
> mind, for the LORD searches all hearts and understands
> every plan and thought. If you seek him, he will be found
> by you, but if you forsake him, he will cast you off forever.
> (1 Chronicles 28:9)

> And I will give them one heart, and a new spirit I will put
> within them. I will remove the heart of stone from their
> flesh and give them a heart of flesh, that they may walk in
> my statutes and keep my rules and obey them. And they
> shall be my people, and I will be their God. But as for
> those whose heart goes after their detestable things and
> their abominations, I will bring their deeds upon their
> own heads, declares the Lord GOD.
> (Ezekiel 11:19-21)

To make it simple I will summarize what these passages say to us.

- First, we long for a heart that desires to love God completely.
- Second, we crave a will that has committed itself to complete obedience to God's will.
- Third, we want a humble and teachable spirit.

All of these things are controlled by our wills. None of these things is possible apart from faith and God's help. None of these things comes naturally to any one of us. Jeremiah reminds us that our fleshly heart is "deceitful above all things, and desperately sick" (Jeremiah 17:9). So don't be discouraged if these things do not come easily or instinctively to you. Join the rest of us!

However, God will be delighted to answer a sincere prayer for His help by granting us these three heartfelt desires.

Here are just a few of the things that we may learn as followers with a passionate heart to do this well.

What Can We Learn as Followers from Both Good and Bad Leaders?

Assuming that we are praying for God to help shape our wills and hearts, here are just a few of the things that we may learn as followers from both kinds of leaders.

My first job after business school was as a General Manager of a failing plant with 150 employees. It was a mess and a daunting assignment. My first boss spent a week with me. He followed me everywhere, never said a word the first four days of the week; he just observed. At the end of the week, he sat me down and critiqued my week. Never have I learned so much in such a short time. He told me, "Bill, if I worked for you, I'd quit."

I was crushed! "Why?" I asked.

He said, "Your standards are too high. You expect perfection too quickly! You have no patience. You are a terrible
encourager!"

Stunned, I sat silently listening.

"Bill, if you spend the rest of your leadership days trying to
be a great encourager, you will never err on the side of being
too encouraging." He was not yelling or animated, just sin-
cerely expressing a criticism he hoped that I listened to.

I came home that night crushed. But I listened, and I have
spent the rest of my leadership trying to encourage. He was
right. I have never gone overboard. In hindsight, I recognize
what a gift these words were to me!

I learned what I should do and how I should do it. I was
severely rebuked, but I listened and I learned. He taught me to
praise in public and rebuke in private. That fits well with the
biblical instruction that public sins are to be dealt with publicly, while private sins are to be dealt with privately.

The Superintendent at the Naval Academy was a wise and
gifted leader. Much needed changing when I was there. I
thought I knew what all of those changes were, and how and
when to incorporate them into the midshipmen's lives. The
Supe listened to me carefully, asked a ton of questions, and
did nothing while I was still a senior. I was disappointed! But
I watched him, as he spent a whole year listening to a lot of
voices, getting a variety of opinions, and carefully cataloguing
each bit of information. To my twenty-one-year-old, impatient
mind he was dawdling, wasting precious time. He was not. He
was carefully assessing the situation before he acted.

To my surprise and pleasure, he acted two months after I
graduated. He implemented a series of improvements that
strengthened the Academy in a well-balanced, sensible, sus-
tainable way. I learned from him that it is best to spend time
in a new situation by carefully evaluating the culture, the circumstances, the strengths, weaknesses, and unfamiliar land-
scapes before boldly acting.

The same lesson can be learned from Nehemiah's actions
before rebuilding the wall of Jerusalem. Nehemiah surveyed

the city carefully before he began his work. This lesson served me well at every turnaround business that I was given to run. We can learn a great deal by osmosis, watching and absorbing truth from good leaders. The apostles had a perfect leader, and they learned a great deal from Jesus. The Gospels and the rest of the New Testament give us an opportunity to apprentice with Christ. We have multiple opportunities to copy the good, imitate what we can, and avoid the pitfalls! Have you studied the Gospels enough to know Jesus well enough to know what to copy and how to do so?

We learn from bad leaders what *not* to do. It is easy and part of human nature to get angry at poor leaders as bosses, to become discouraged, disheartened, and to find reasons to quit or check out silently—and possibly even develop a hatred for them. This applies to poor Christian leaders as well. Surprise, surprise! Not all Christian leaders are good ones! John tells us that if we hate our brother in Christ, then we are murderers (see 1 John 3:15). So when you have a pathetic boss who gets almost everything wrong, forgive him and learn from him. Learn what not to do! Samson was a strong man but a weak leader. Saul was a big man, a handsome man, but a very flawed leader. David was an incredibly accomplished warrior, a gifted poet, and yet a miserable father. We can learn what not to do from these men.

Pray that God would help you to avoid the mistakes you have seen when you have the opportunity to lead. The apostles watched Jesus deal with poor Jewish leaders. However, He never hated them! He rebuked them in love and with strictness at times because they were bullheaded like many of us. People learned from these poor leaders what not to do and from Jesus how to oppose untruth with grace and courage. Often this sort of action was costly, so it may also be for us!

The question for each of us is this: "How do I react to an inept boss?"

What Can We Learn from Circumstances?

Being a good follower has benefits. There is less disciplinary trouble to suffer, as well as advancement, privileges, learning, real living, joyful obedience, and honor.

Circumstances teach us that there are some things that can be controlled, but there are many more things that are completely out of our control. Being in Christ helps enable us to discern the difference between those things that are controllable and those that are not. Circumstances give us opportunities to make mistakes. Will we react with confidence and biblical truth to the things that we have a say in, and accept the things out of our control and leave the results to God? Or will we pout like Jonah did when God behaved in a manner that did not suit Jonah?

The apostles certainly experienced a myriad of challenging circumstances. They could not control the Roman governors or the Jewish leadership, but they could control their speech! They could not control the jailers who chained and beat them, but they could control their prayers and hymn singing. They could not control the persecution that broke out against them, but they could control their response to the Spirit instructing them to scatter.

Summary

All proper mature Christian leaders begin the same way—as followers. Even those who have been given exceptional natural leadership gifts must start as followers. Why? Because although they may be blessed with unsurpassed worldly leadership talents, they may yet have no clue about what the Bible has to say concerning how to use those gifts. They must learn and assimilate knowledge before they can become a Christian leader. Learning takes time, practice, mistakes, correction, and critique. Teaching and experience are prerequisites for learning. Even Jesus was an experiential learner—see Hebrews 5:8. Until the day of his death, a Christian leader's learning never stops.

The primary obstacle for a follower to develop into a godly leader is his will. The will is that part of us that has the ability to choose. The will is like a rheostat. As mentioned in chapter 17, a rheostat is a variable dimmer switch. The dining rooom lights could be on full power or dimmed to darkness. Our will can regulate the intensity of our spiritual growth just as a dimmer switch regulates light. Choosing whom to listen to, whom to imitate, how much to commit, what to read, how long to study, or whether to allow distractions to lead us to evil or minutia involve a critical function of our will. Those decisions control our growth and maturity as Christian leaders. The Spirit of God is with us to teach and guide our will, but our will must learn submission to the Spirit's leading. That submission does not come instinctively and it often comes grudgingly.

So, if you aspire to leadership, just remember "Leaders begin as *followers.*" It is no shame to be a follower. Following is God's pathway to biblically informed and consistent leadership. Good followers make good leaders!

Get started.

B

Be Submissive

And Hezekiah prayed to the LORD: "O LORD of hosts, God of Israel, enthroned above the cherubim, you are the God, you alone, of all the kingdoms of the earth; you have made heaven and earth."
Isaiah 37:15–16

The fear of the LORD is the beginning of wisdom; all those who practice it have a good understanding.
His praise endures forever!
Psalm 111:10

My Harvard Business School professor might give me a "low pass" for making this the second point of importance for a Christian leader. I will leave that to him. However, to God, this trait is extraordinarily important.

Submissiveness is not easy for any of us. Our flesh wants to have its own way. My flesh, your flesh, everyone's flesh! There are no exceptions.

When I say, "Be submissive," I mean be submissive to God. When? First! Last! Always! No matter where you are, no matter what position you are in. Why? Because God is our ultimate authority, no matter how many human superiors we may have. God is final! Solomon in Ecclesiastes says it this way,

> If you see in a province the oppression of the poor and the
> violation of justice and righteousness, do not be amazed
> at the matter, for the high official is watched by a higher,
> and there are yet higher ones over them.
> (Eccl. 5:8)

Solomon is reminding us that, in the chain of command, there is always a more superior Boss—God! This fact is quite easy to forget in the heat of a challenging moment—even for Christians, maybe even *especially* for Christians. We know we are meant to be dependent upon God. We trust in God's power and protection. However, we can be lured into a false sense of security and then suddenly immersed in life-threatening circumstances. In such a situation, it is easy to overlook our moorings, and forget!

It is even easier to drift upon a dangerous, destructive tide. C. S. Lewis once wrote that few of us set out to sin. Rather, more often than not, we make little compromises, little lapses in memory of truth, little steps in the wrong direction. Our life courses can, little by little, veer into hazardous territory.

But, no matter what, God should always be our last and final authority, and our heart attitude should always be one of submission to His Word and His guidance. With judgment day in mind, we ought honestly to ask ourselves if this is true in every closet of our lives.

My first job after business school was in Boise, Idaho. We moved our household 2,700 miles away from Boston with two children, bought a home, and settled in for what we assumed would be a long career. I went into work the first day, dressed in my best suit, ready to conquer the world. My boss was a Senior Vice President of a Fortune 500 company and I was promised a general management assignment in one year. Hopes were high; the salary was good; the future looked bright! Then, my boss called me into his office and gave me my first assignment. Things changed very rapidly!

> Bill, I want you to call our primary competitor, and pretend that you are a customer. I then want you to place a tentative sham order so that we may obtain all the pricing information on these thirty products. We need to see how our products stack up and compete. I would like this information by the end of the day. Is that clear?

I responded as any junior associate might, "Yes, sir!" I closed the door and left his office returning to my cubicle, thinking that sounded easy.

As I looked up the phone number of the distributor I was instructed to call, I began to think more deeply about the assignment I had just been given. On the surface, it seemed simple enough and quite harmless. "All's fair in love and war and cutthroat competition." Right?

Yet, I had been the head of the Honor Committee at the

Naval Academy. How would we have looked at someone who completed this task? Favorably? No! Not on your life! We would have booted the culprit out of school, wouldn't we? I was being asked to deliberately mislead, wasn't I? "Is this circumstance different and justified," I asked myself? "If so, why and how?" Suddenly a simple assignment did not seem so simple.

My boss had asked me to lie, to pretend to be someone I was not, and hoodwink our competing company into giving me information beneficial to us and detrimental to them. That was just unethical. I was not yet a believer, but I did have enough Bible knowledge, common grace, and fear of the Lord to know that "lying" and "deceit" were not good things. I took pride in telling the truth, and I pressed myself to answer, "How would this assignment fit with what I wanted to be?" Did I want a reputation as a good liar? Looking back on it now, without my knowing it, God had used the experiences of my life at home, at the Academy, and at church to drive home the fact that there was a higher authority than my boss and a natural law that supplanted human judgments. This stopped me dead in my tracks. My mind began to race. My emotions were energized as I found myself thinking such thoughts as these:

- "I am going to get fired on my first day at work!"
- "I can't lie, I shouldn't lie, and yet I told my boss I understood his assignment and that I would get the job done! How do I get out of that honorably and without punishment?"
- "I can't be one of those guys who can't get anything done!" My pride was counterattacking me!
- "I moved my family out to Idaho, 2,700 miles from Boston, 1,600 miles from Texas, our home state. What have I done?"

Thankfully, panic left me. Rational consideration returned. I had a task to complete. There had to be alternative ways to obtain the information needed. Weren't there? If so, what were those alternative methods? I thought for quite some time about different paths that I might take. God was gracious and led me to a solution that would provide the results I needed. I still had to inform my boss.

I went back into his office, worried that he might be angry with my dilemma, and said, "Boss, I could not call the distributor and lie. But I have found a different way to obtain the information we need without false pretense. Are you okay with that?"

His answer was short, gruff, and a bit surprised: "Okay! Okay! Just so we get the information! Get it!"

I think he was shocked to hear I thought he had asked me to lie! I also was operating at a level of detail he was not concerned with, certainly a level of ethics that was not on his radar. He just wanted to beat the competitor soundly, any way he could!

I acted the way that I did because I knew that I needed to be submissive to a higher authority than my boss!

The important thing for Christian leaders is this: God wants God's work done God's way. That means that even if we are Christians in secular businesses, there is a way that we are meant to decide, act, and perform. That way is in conformity with God's Word, His heart, His principles, His ethics. This does not mean we are meant to be little toy soldiers, woodenly marching in lockstep. God has given us great creativity and imagination, but His way is always defined and bounded by the plumb line of His Word, the Bible.

We may have worldly bosses, but we also have a "Big Boss" who supersedes all others. Our behaviors, all of them, are ultimately accountable to Him, and to Him alone. Paul says it this way to the Colossian church:

> And whatever you do, in word or deed, do everything
> in the name of the Lord Jesus, giving thanks to God the
> Father through him.
> (Col. 3:17)

This instruction is not just for pastors. It is not just for Sundays. It is for all of life—24/7! It is for every industry. It is for every profession. It is for government workers, sole proprietors, artists, writers, politicians. It is for every Christian in every walk of life.

The Nazi leaders under Hitler would have done well to listen to the theology of the Lutheran pastor, Dietrich Bonhoeffer. They have answered ultimately to God! The accountants at Arthur Anderson would still be in business if they had listened to God instead of pragmatism about ENRON. The crew of the space shuttle *Challenger* would still be alive if the executives at Morton Thiokol and NASA had remembered that we all answer to Almighty God.

If we want to endure and finish strong as Christian leaders, it is incumbent upon us to remember that we all ought to be submissive to OUR CREATOR. In fact, we will be accountable for that submissiveness whether we obey Him or not! Hence, the second note of encouragement is this: "Be submissive."

C

Be a Student of Biblical Leaders

Have this mind among yourselves, which is yours in Christ Jesus, who, though he was in the form of God, did not count equality with God a thing to be grasped, but made himself nothing, taking the form of a servant, being born in the likeness of men. And being found in human form, he humbled himself by becoming obedient to the point of death, even death on a cross.
Philippians 2:5–8

When we think of leaders, we normally call to mind people we have known, people we have served under, people we have read about, military leaders, sports team leaders, political leaders, and pastoral leaders like Billy Graham, John Calvin, the Wesley brothers, Augustine, and Martin Luther. We seldom think to pull out our Old Testament or New Testament and point to a certain man or woman or circumstance. I am encouraging us to reconsider our normal way of thinking!

Years ago when I was taking a seminary class on Old Testament Survey at a remote campus in Akron, Ohio, Professor Willem VanGemeren (the instructor) and I struck up a friendship. We stayed in the same hotel, because the class met over a weekend and he had to fly in from Chicago, while I had to drive from Cleveland. We would have breakfast together and talk about ministry, our families, and the class. Willem was an absolute delight to speak with!

One morning, we turned to the subject of a class I was teaching at my company on leadership based on the book of Nehemiah. I was using material provided by Walt Wiley titled *The Look of the Leader*. I was enthusing about how good the material was and relating to Willem the men's reactions and growth.

"Willem, the men seem to be getting a lot of practical advice from the material. They relate well to Nehemiah's situation that could be described as a 'dog's breakfast'—a complete mess—a tragedy for God's people," I said.

I expected Willem to join in the adulation of the learning that was taking place concerning Nehemiah and leadership. I was sorely mistaken!

Willem responded very gruffly and with passion in his reply: "Nehemiah was a terrible leader. He was a blight on the idea of godly leadership, and I wish you were teaching leadership using some other example!"

It took me a moment to regain my composure because his response was so much different than I had expected. I am absolutely certain I do not remember all of his arguments against poor Nehemiah, and I am also certain that they were cogent, well developed, and solidly biblical. The two arguments I do remember were these:

First, Nehemiah physically threatened some Jewish leaders and physically disciplined others. The Bible says that he pulled their hair out. Willem had a beard and he interpreted that verse to say that Nehemiah pulled their beard hair out. He was appalled at Nehemiah's physical abuse.

Second, he argued, "The best example of leadership in the Bible is Jesus!"

I responded to this, saying, "Jesus is the best example of everything—leadership, speaking, praying, following, teaching, etc. I cannot argue against that statement! But does that mean we cannot learn from other men in the Bible? Which one of them was perfect like Jesus?"

He said, "We should learn first and foremost from Jesus! And there are better examples of leadership to use than Nehemiah."

After several morning debates, we agreed to disagree about Nehemiah. But I had to admit that there is no better example of leadership than Jesus!

Jesus, as an example of leadership, presents some unique problems for today's teachers of leadership. During His lifetime, He never created an organization, He wrote no books, established no schools, never made much money, never wrote anything that we have for posterity, posited no formal declaration of vision, goals, values, culture, strategy, or key performance indicators. Yet we ought never forget what Willem said: "The best example of leadership in the Bible is Jesus!"

If we aspire to be Christian leaders, and by that I do not mean just a leader in a church, NGO, or parachurch organization. I mean any man who wants to be a fully devoted follower of Jesus Christ in any industry known to man, in any field. If we aspire to be Christian leaders, then we should be knowledgeable students of biblical leaders, especially Jesus.

Here are some questions we should be able to answer and be able to turn to a Bible book, chapter, and verse in order to orient ourselves properly.

- How and why did Adam fail as the first leader?
- What can we learn from Lamech?
- What things did Noah do well, and where did he go wrong?
- Abraham was a leader. What did he do well?
- What did Abraham do poorly?
- Do we know where Abraham failed, faltered, and compromised? Why?
- How can we imitate Abraham's courage and avoid his incredibly poor judgment at times?
- What can you learn from Abraham about the influence of circumstances on a leader's judgment?
- How did Isaac follow in his father's footsteps?
- Can you identify the strengths and weaknesses of Jacob?
- How could Joseph be a faithful follower of God and yet also work for a pagan boss?

These questions come from just one book—Genesis. These men's lives are real biographies that we are meant to learn from. Some commentators consider that these characters and others are just folklore, myths, fairy tales, stories that have been made up to illustrate moral niceties. Poppycock! Don't miss the joy and learning which is there to be had from the actual history of human beings just like us.

Have you ever looked for a challenging leadership book that will provide you with real-life advice on how to manage a large group of people over an extended period of time? Exodus is the ticket! Do you like war stories? Joshua and Judges give you good examples and pathetic examples of characters placed in positions of leadership in war. If you think America is in bad shape and needs some reconstruction, try Ezra and Nehemiah. Do you feel like everything in the world is against you and nothing is going right, and no one, not even your wife, is on your side, then you can't go wrong with Job.

I hope that you get the idea. Every book in the Bible teaches us some aspect of leadership. Some books reflect good leadership habits; others expose poor behaviors. Some men in the Bible are downright rotten! In all there are sixty-six books with varied cultures, contexts, and problems. Being familiar with all these biblical leaders is the next best thing to actual experience. If you want to aspire to Christian leadership, become a student of biblical leaders. The more that you know of their mistakes, the fewer mistakes you will make. The more you understand and learn concerning the good examples of leadership in Scripture, the more you will encounter smooth sailing.

D

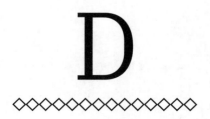

Be Holy

You shall be holy to me, for I the Lord am holy and have separated you from the peoples, that you should be mine.
Leviticus 20:26

Have you ever gone to a nice restaurant and seen a menu like this?

Today's Specials!
◇◇◇◇◇◇◇◇◇◇◇◇◇◇◇◇◇◇◇◇◇◇◇◇◇◇◇◇

- Rotten apple pie $6
- Rancid beef tenderloin $20
- Moldy croissants $5 each
- Sour milk $3 a glass

The thought is ridiculous. But the idea of a corrupted menu like this pales in comparison to a Christian leader who is described by all those that he leads as unholy, lacking integrity, and being a liar and a womanizer.

All Christians are called to be holy as God is holy. This requirement is particularly important for Christian leaders in the church. 1 Timothy 3:1–13 and Titus 1:5–9 give God's requirements for elders and deacons. We would do well to read those passages, heed the advice that God gives to Timothy and Titus through the apostle Paul, and apply them, not just to leaders in the church, but to all Christian leaders. In very practical, understandable language, God fleshes out what it means to be holy as He is holy in these two passages.

I cannot improve upon what Paul says by the Spirit. What I can do is discuss briefly our human difficulty with understanding and applying the words "Be holy as I am holy," and then point out two everyday aspects of holiness in Christian leadership that these requirements implicitly produce: the fact of loneliness; and the need for genuineness.

Our Human Difficulty with Holiness

The basic meaning of holiness is *otherness*. When we apply that to God, most of us can see right away God's *otherness*. He is omnipotent. No human being is omnipotent, so to be holy as God is holy cannot mean that we are to attempt to be all-powerful in ways such as He is.

He is omnipresent. That means He is able to be everywhere all at once. Can we do that if we try really hard? We all know the answer to that. Here is a short abbreviated list of some of God's other attributes.

- Immutability
- Infinity
- Simplicity
- Knowledge
- Goodness
- Love
- Grace
- Mercy
- Long-suffering
- Holiness
- Righteousness
- Veracity
- Sovereignty

Take a look at this list and, with each one, ask yourself, "Could I ever, be holy as God is holy in this attribute?" The answer is a definite "No!" There is not one chance in a million that any of us could be holy as God is holy. Never in a million lifetimes could we strive to be *other* as God is *other* in even a single attribute. If we are honest and thinking, we find that we are astounded at God's *otherness*, and we are equally convinced of our own commonness and our lack of separation from evil.

Yet most of us are quite adept at giving our Sunday School answer, "I am to be holy as God is holy" and at the same time not having a clue as to what it really means to be holy as God is holy.

Two Everyday Aspects of Holiness in Christian Leadership

Here are a few thoughts. This is not meant to be exhaustive. It is merely meant to help us with our understanding of what it means for us as mortals to be holy. Let's start with two basics.

LONENESS

If you want to become holy, prepare to be lonely. Expectations play a big part in how we act and react. If you are going to lead and be holy, there are times when you will be alone. Expect it. It will not be all the time, but it will also not be seldom.

One of the downsides of being a leader is loneliness. The old saying "It is lonely at the top" is true. Every pastor knows this and experiences loneliness. Every CEO, general manager, supervisor, and parent experiences loneliness as well. Loneliness is one of the main reasons why pastors burn out. Loneliness comes with the territory. Fathers would do well to pay close attention to this illustration.

Our daughter went to a very good high school. My wife and I attended a meeting of parents of the freshman class. The topics of discussion were moral issues concerning our sons and daughters.

- What should we as parents do about allowing our children to attend "R rated" movies?
- Should we limit our children's consumption of alcohol and, if so, how?
- Can we as parents do anything to mitigate premarital sex and, if so, how?

About fifty parents were in attendance. There was discussion of each issue and a vote at the end approving the agreed-upon solution. On each issue the vote was forty-six for the proposal and four against. My wife and I and one other couple were the only dissenters among the group. We gave our opinions and were quite alone. Few parents even listened to our opinions. To the others in attendance, we were viewed as outdated, outmoded morons, completely ignorant of the century and culture in which we lived.

Their solutions were:

- PROBLEM: What should we as parents do about allowing our children to attend "R rated" movies?
- SOLUTION. It was deemed foolish to try to prevent kids from attending "R rated" movies. It was a waste of time. So, let 'em go!

- PROBLEM: Should we limit our children's consumption of alcohol and, if so, how?
- SOLUTION: Provide alcohol in the home so that kids did not have to drive to obtain alcohol and did not have to drive home after drinking.

- PROBLEM: Can we as parents do anything to mitigate premarital sex and, if so, how?
- SOLUTION: There is nothing we can do to prevent premarital sex. What we can do is provide a safe and secure bedroom in our homes so our kids do not have to sneak around or use the back seat of a car.

The point is we were alone in being leaders in our role as parents both at the meeting and then when we came home. We heard quite often from our daughter, "I am the only person at school who cannot go to an 'R' rated movie!" To be holy as a parent will require loneliness. When and how it will come I cannot say, but it will come if you are being a godly parent.

Pastors know and feel loneliness when they are called by

the scriptural text to preach a sermon that they know will cause their congregation to bristle. Discipline of members, staff, and friends is a lonely pursuit, seldom with kudos or occasions of encouragement. The privilege of leadership in the church comes with great joy and great opportunities for discouragement, for the pastor and the pastor alone. Derek Prime captures the essence of aloneness and the joy of ministry, alongside the accompanying occasions of discouragement.

> While Paul could write, "Now we really live, since you are standing firm in the Lord" (1 Thessalonians 3:8), he knew the opposite emotion when believers wavered and went backwards. God's people have a unique capacity to sweeten or spoil our days, to thrill us or to cast us into the depths of depression. One moment we may feel that there is no other place to be but where we are; and the next we wish we could be anywhere else. People may listen carefully to what we say, as we faithfully declare the truth of the gospel, and then choose to turn away. "Have I now become your enemy," Paul wrote to the Galatians, "by telling you the truth?"[1]

Notice Paul says, "I have become your enemy," not, "We have become your enemy!" He is alone in his despair.

As CEO of several companies, I have had to fire numerous people. Firing folks has never been a joy, and it has never been a group event. The decision to have to lay off good people, hardworking people, is never easy and it is never done with a cheering crowd. Tasks like these are lonely.

At my first business, every test machine we sold was outfitted with a personal computer. After traveling with sales people for six months and listening to customers, I decided to move the entire company from one brand of personal computer to another. Why? Because ninety percent of our customers used the new brand. Not a soul in my company agreed—not the COO, not the engineers, not the sales force. They all loved the

1 Derek Prime, *Pastors and Teachers* (Highland Books, 1989), 256.

old product. No one agreed with me! I was alone in the decision, and yet it spurred the next ten years of successes, providing another one hundred jobs in our company. Years later, everyone saw it as pivotal to our growth, but at the time it was viewed as stupid. It was a lonely decision, but a necessary one!

Henry Ford was alone in believing an affordable car could be produced. Steve Jobs was alone in believing that a phone could do more than connect two people in a conversation.

Husbands are also not immune from aloneness. We married our wives to be in a relationship with a woman whom we deeply love. That relationship is precious, valuable, and treasured. However, there will also be moments when you as a husband must stand alone to be holy in the sight of God. On that occasion, you may have to say something like this to your wife.

> Honey, I love you very much. There is not a bone in my body that desires to do anything that divides us. I have listened to you. You are a great blessing to me and you fill in my blind spots. However, today I must listen to how God is leading me in a different direction than you think is right. I hope you will understand and submit graciously. I cannot control that and I will not try. But even if you can't, know that I answer first, foremost, and ultimately to God for our family, and not to you.

The point is this: Christian leaders in any discipline, industry, or profession who want to be holy will have plenty of opportunities to be alone. Attempting to lead in a Christian way, a biblical way, and a holy way will often create conflict. In the face of that conflict, Christian leaders need to be ready and equipped to be alone.

The antidote for loneliness is simple. It is to remember that God is always present in us by His Spirit. As a believer, you are never really alone! I once heard that the definition of a majority is this: "One person plus God is a majority!" There is a lot of truth in this statement, and believing it will do much to prepare us for the loneliness that is sure to come.

GENUINENESS

To be holy we need to be genuine. Genuineness has two aspects related to holiness. The first is that our speech must genuinely match our example. The second is that we must have genuine knowledge of our God.

Speech must align with example. Leaders lead by precept and example. Precepts are teachings. They are verbally expressed. They are speech. They are guidelines, principles, goals, methods, values, beliefs, and methods which we, as leaders, express passionately and often to our people. They are often spoken, many times written down in a handbook or employee manual, and subsequently printed in a company's annual report to shareholders.

Our people hear these messages and then they watch us to see if what we say squares with what we do. Is our example living out the precepts that we have taught? That is the question that every associate is consciously or unconsciously asking every day. They are watching our example! Are our precepts being lived out in our daily lives together? When the precepts do not align with the example, trouble is afoot. When they align, the sailing will be smoother.

Every parent knows this truth. A child learns as much (if not more) from what their parents do as they do from what their parents say. In simple language, our walk needs to match our talk. We did the same thing when we were children; we listened to our parents and then watched how they lived—there was precept and example.

Most of us have experienced a leader who said one thing and did a completely different thing. I have been on several company boards in my career. One company I served had a CEO who was directing everyone in the company that thrift was needed. "Every penny counted, watch every expenditure," he barked. He squeezed and squeezed everyone except himself. When he went to conferences, he stayed in five-star hotels, dined at the finest restaurants, ordered limousines, and flew first class. There's nothing wrong with any of those things in and of themselves, but to advise and expect frugality from everyone else, and yet live in opulence himself, was his downfall. He did not last and was not successful. He professed to be a Christian but his speech did not align with his example. To be holy is to be genuine—our speech should align with our life.

The second part of genuineness is that we must know the genuine God, not some partial creation of our own making. Authentic, truthful knowledge is paramount!

I am told that T-Men who search out counterfeiters of U.S. dollars spend the majority of their time becoming experts on knowing every minute detail of each denomination of U.S. currency. They spend hours upon hours observing each element of a printed bill—the type style, the colors of ink being used, the paper, and its makeup. As they become accomplished sleuths, knowing every detail of our paper money, they become effective agents.

The same is true of us as Christian leaders. If we want to be holy Christian leaders, we need to become experts in identifying the real God, the real Jesus, the real Spirit. The way to do that is twofold: we must pray and we must study.

First we ought to pray that God would open the eyes of our hearts and reveal Himself to us. By using the term *hearts,* I mean the convergence of our intellects, our emotions, and our wills. So we ask God to open our hearts and then fill them with a hunger and thirst for Him.

> Oh, taste and see that the LORD is good!
> (Ps. 34:8)

That hunger and thirst can only be satisfied by gorging ourselves on God's Word. Therefore, we pray for God's help and we pray for a healthy appetite.

So if the first step is to pray, the second step is to study. Learning can only come from the *discipline* of learning. Time invested and using the proper study methods are the simple recipe for maturation. The motivation for this should be our love for God and the importance of the privilege we have been given. To be a Christian leader who is holy is a great privilege and honor. However it is also a hallowed responsibility. Why? Because the honor and glory of the God who saved us, blessed us, and gave us life is at stake. The reputation of our Sovereign is in our hands with the people whom we lead. It is important! God entrusts this duty to us as leaders. We should want to study to honor the privilege that we have been given.

Being a naval aviator was serious business for me. Every flight was an opportunity to learn and have our skills tested. However, every flight was also an opportunity to die. A failed hydraulic system, a flame out of an engine, a malfunctioning electrical system—any one of those failures could result in death. To prepare for those emergencies, we had a book that was a thousand pages long. It was not bedtime reading. It explained each system, how it functioned, and what to do in the case of a failure. We studied this book because our lives depended upon it. We had a hunger for it because it was indispensable.

We should have that same hunger for God's Word. It is important to our development as holy Christian leaders. Without it, we are flying on our own, and that is risky business for us and those whom we lead. God's Word covers life from conception to burial, and it covers marriage, divorce, finance, borrowing, discipline, love, and respect—and many more topics. Very few things are absent in the biblical narrative.

Summary

If we want to be holy Christian leaders, we want to be described by the people we lead as men who love God, who lead in a biblical manner, who walk consistently with our talk, who set an example of integrity, who tell the truth even when it reflects poorly on us, and are men who love God's people in a way that is as near as possible to a Christlike love.

It is difficult to understand what God means when He says, "Be holy as I am holy," but we can do our best to read 1 Timothy and Titus and seek to become what Paul encourages us to be. We can prepare ourselves for the inevitability of loneliness and put on the life jacket of prayer. We can strive to become genuine Christian leaders whose walks resemble our talks and whose God is authentic and genuine—the God presented to us in the Bible.

About Shepherd Press Publications

They are gospel driven.
They are heart focused.
They are life changing.

Our Invitation to You

We passionately believe that what we are publishing can be of benefit to you, your family, your friends, and your work colleagues. So we are inviting you to join our online mailing list so that we may reach out to you with news about our latest and forthcoming publications, and with special offers.

Visit:

www.shepherdpress.com/newsletter

and provide your name and email address.